DREW PAUTZ

Drew Pautz was born and brought up in Canada and now lives in London. His first play *Someone Else's Shoes* premiered at Soho Theatre in 2007. From 2003–2007 he was a founder member of The Work Theatre Collective, dedicated to collaboratively created performance. Drew has also worked extensively as a lighting designer for theatre and dance, as well as an occasional director of theatre and short film.

Other Titles in this Series

Alecky Blythe
CRUISING
THE GIRLFRIEND EXPERIENCE

Andrew Bovell
SPEAKING IN TONGUES
WHEN THE RAIN STOPS FALLING

Jez Butterworth
JERUSALEM
MOJO
THE NIGHT HERON
PARLOUR SONG
THE WINTERLING

Alexi Kaye Campbell
APOLOGIA
THE PRIDE

Caryl Churchill
BLUE HEART
CHURCHILL PLAYS: THREE
CHURCHILL PLAYS: FOUR
CHURCHILL: SHORTS
CLOUD NINE
A DREAM PLAY *after* Strindberg
DRUNK ENOUGH TO SAY
     I LOVE YOU?
FAR AWAY
HOTEL
ICECREAM
LIGHT SHINING IN
     BUCKINGHAMSHIRE
MAD FOREST
A NUMBER
SEVEN JEWISH CHILDREN
THE SKRIKER
THIS IS A CHAIR
THYESTES *after* Seneca
TRAPS

Stella Feehily
DREAMS OF VIOLENCE
DUCK
O GO MY MAN

Declan Feenan
ST PETERSBURG *and other plays*

debbie tucker green
BORN BAD
DIRTY BUTTERFLY
RANDOM
STONING MARY
TRADE & GENERATIONS

Joel Horwood
FOOD *with* Christopher Heimann
I CAUGHT CRABS
     IN WALBERSWICK
STOOPUD FUCKEN ANIMALS

Fin Kennedy
HOW TO DISAPPEAR
     COMPLETELY AND NEVER
     BE FOUND
PROTECTION

Lucy Kirkwood
HEDDA *after* Ibsen
IT FELT EMPTY WHEN THE
     HEART WENT AT FIRST BUT
     IT IS ALRIGHT NOW
TINDERBOX

Conor McPherson
DUBLIN CAROL
McPHERSON: FOUR PLAYS
McPHERSON PLAYS: TWO
PORT AUTHORITY
THE SEAFARER
SHINING CITY
THE WEIR

Chloë Moss
CHRISTMAS IS MILES AWAY
HOW LOVE IS SPELT
THIS WIDE NIGHT
THE WAY HOME

Joanna Murray Smith
BOMBSHELLS
THE FEMALE OF THE SPECIES
HONOUR

Ali Taylor
COTTON WOOL
OVERSPILL

Jack Thorne
2ND MAY 1997
STACY & FANNY AND FAGGOT
WHEN YOU CURE ME

Enda Walsh
BEDBOUND & MISTERMAN
DELIRIUM
DISCO PIGS &
     SUCKING DUBLIN
THE NEW ELECTRIC BALLROOM
THE SMALL THINGS
THE WALWORTH FARCE

Drew Pautz

LOVE THE SINNER

NICK HERN BOOKS

London

www.nickhernbooks.co.uk

A Nick Hern Book

Love the Sinner first published in Great Britain as a paperback original in 2010 by Nick Hern Books Limited, 14 Larden Road, London W3 7ST

Love the Sinner copyright © 2010 Drew Pautz

Drew Pautz has asserted his right to be identified as the author of this work

Cover image by Image Werks/Corbis
Cover designed by Ned Hoste, 2H
Typeset by Nick Hern Books, London
Printed in the UK by CLE Print Ltd, St Ives, Cambs, PE27 3LE

A CIP catalogue record for this book is available from the British Library

ISBN   978 1 84842 089 2

Love the Sinner was first performed in the Cottesloe auditorium of the National Theatre, London, on 11 May 2010 (previews from 4 May) with the following cast:

JOSEPH	Fiston Barek
JOHN /	Paul Bentall
REVEREND FARLEY	
HANNAH / ALISON	Nancy Crane
MICHAEL	Jonathan Cullen
TOM / BILL	Sam Graham
MATTHEW / HARRY	Robert Gwilym
DANIEL	Scott Handy
JAMES / DAVE	Fraser James
PAUL	Louis Mahoney
SHELLY	Charlotte Randle
STEPHEN	Ian Redford
SIMON/OFFICIAL	Richard Rees

Director	Matthew Dunster
Designer	Anna Fleischle
Lighting Designer	Philip Gladwell
Music	Jules Maxwell
Sound Designer	Paul Arditti

Characters

THE PRIMATES

Where nationality is not noted represent as international a group as possible

STEPHEN, *British*
PAUL, *African*
JAMES, *African*
JOHN, *Australian*
HANNAH, *North American*
SIMON, *North American*
MATTHEW
TOM

DANIEL, *British, secretary*
JOSEPH, *African, young, hotel porter*

MICHAEL, *British, forty-two*
SHELLY, *British, his wife, thirty-nine*

EMPLOYEES OF MICHAEL'S ENVELOPE COMPANY

ALISON
HARRY
DAVE
BILL

REVEREND FARLEY
CONGREGANTS, OFFICIALS, PHOTOGRAPHER, etc.

Primates, employees, congregants and officials may double

This text went to press before the end of rehearsals and so may differ slightly from the play as performed.

Notes on the Text

Lines frequently overlap and several 'conversations' or asides occur simultaneously. At times everyone may speak at once, or nearly, and occasionally this means a full page may (and often should) pass very quickly. Where the text is laid out in columns it is to assist the logic of who is simultaneously speaking or reacting to whom – it approximates when overlaps begin and end, exact pacing will only be found in production. Those who are not speaking are, of course, also part of general reactions. The density of text is thus sometimes misleading, and the argument is as often in the rhythm or 'cacophony' as in the words.

The symbols * and (occasionally) ^ are used to help find where lines 'cut into' simultaneous conversations and/or to what line of dialogue or expression a character may be reacting. Regular parenthesis (   ) around a line indicate that the line is either an 'aside' to another character or delivered in a register different from the dominant conversation. A forward slash / indicates where a following line interrupts and overlaps.

The time is the present.

The characters are all fictional.

Author's Note

Thank you to everyone at the National Theatre and all those who offered time and insight during the play's long journey to the stage. Very special thanks to Chris Campbell, Sebastian Born, Joe Phillips, Matthew Dunster… and to *Gitta*, always.

1

Night. A hotel conference room. A small pile of money on a table.

Conference badges.

DANIEL. Okay, I think we're confused.

Let me check this again.

JAMES. Didn't you write it down?

DANIEL. Four regular Americanos two with sugar*

MATTHEW. Six?

JAMES. I didn't want sugar

DANIEL. Two of the four** –

John did. Two others with cream

JAMES. (It doesn't really matter)

DANIEL. Two cappuccino two lattes.

STEPHEN. **I'm tea

Tea. Thank you.

With milk. Please.

DANIEL. I know.

TOM. (Jesus)

MATTHEW. (Tom, how many times do I have to ask you)

TOM. (I don't believe this)

JOHN. *Americanos?

SIMON. Regular coffee

HANNAH. It's just normal coffee

SIMON. That's what they call it

JOHN. 'Americano'

SIMON. Like 'Grande'. What's wrong with 'large'?

JOHN. Call a spade a spade, eh?

SIMON. Well, exactly, I guess

JOHN. Slippery, isn't it?

STEPHEN. No sugar.

DANIEL. I know

PAUL. And I will have a water, please, Daniel. If I may.

DANIEL. Water? Instead, or as well as – ?

JAMES. I will have water too.

PAUL. Oh, as well as. Always a small glass of water with coffee, like in Italy.

DANIEL. Okay.

JOHN. Me too, actually.

DANIEL. Right.

MATTHEW. Count me in.

TOM. (Well, I'll have water too then.)

STEPHEN. Shall we all have water?

HANNAH. Yes.

DANIEL. I can get a pitcher.

TOM. (Always the flourish)

SIMON. (Practically Catholic.)

But raising his hand to be included.

I'll have a water.

STEPHEN. That's an excellent idea, Daniel, yes. Thank you. Good.

DANIEL. And everyone's paid? / (*Checking with him.*) Michael?

HANNAH. Yes.

Some grumbles, other 'yeses'.

STEPHEN. (We should be okay, Daniel)

DANIEL. I'm sorry we're into our per diems at this stage, gentlemen – Hannah

MICHAEL. (Oh, I don't know, I think so)

SIMON. Who knows, this currency is impossible.

TOM *and* SIMON *put money in.*

PAUL. I think so.

STEPHEN. (Yes… fine.)

MATTHEW. There should be 30,000.

STEPHEN. Yes? Good.
  Excellent.

  Now.

  Little pause.

  Back to business.

  Paragraph 18.2.2

  Pause.

DANIEL (*very quietly into phone*). Four Americanos, please. Two with sugar, two with cream. Two cappuccinos. Two lattes, please. And a tea. Two teas. Yes. Yes. Yes. And a pitcher of water. A large pitcher. Yes. Thank you.

All wait with anticipation for the next item of business…

STEPHEN. Paul?

PAUL (*beat*). No. It is wrong.

Explosion of reaction. Compressed responses, simultaneous, overlapping cacophony.

TOM. Oh…!

STEPHEN. Paul, please

PAUL. *No.**

DANIEL. Okay…

STEPHEN. Just consider

JOHN (*in opposition to* HANNAH *and* SIMON). No. It's suicidal… No way.

PAUL. I would like to explain myself.

SIMON. It's offensive^

HANNAH. This is nonsense*

SIMON. Idiotic! We're not asking *you* to change

MATTHEW. I think I under-stand

JAMES (*in agreement with* PAUL).** We are crystal clear on this…

MATTHEW. There is a logic.

TOM. It's ridiculous

MATTHEW. Well

JAMES. ^Offensive?

DANIEL. Stop stop stop
please!

STEPHEN. Please.

Little pause.

We're very close. There is a solution for all of us – We're
also very tired. If I suggested another short break,

consider, wait for the
coffee – yes. Now. Then
perhaps we'll crack it.

PAUL. Now?

JAMES. Consider what?

JOHN. Why?

SIMON. (We don't know
how else to explain…)

PAUL. This is the very problem, the exact problem right here.

TOM. Taking a break?

PAUL. This is what you propose?

STEPHEN. Because we are tired.

TOM. Yes

MATTHEW. (Shattered)

PAUL. Two stags are fighting. As one wears the other down,
neither proposes a break to catch his breath. His opponent
would laugh, spear him in the belly.

SIMON. You're laughing?

PAUL. I am telling a story.

MATTHEW. We're just tired.

PAUL. I am not tired.

TOM. (You're lucky)

STEPHEN. We're not fighting.

PAUL. I am committed.

SIMON. (Is he always like this?)

JOHN. Sorry?   JAMES. Like what?

SIMON. Nothing.

PAUL. No, please. You think I am like something. I would like to know what that is.

Everyone's attention.

SIMON. It's a figure of speech.

PAUL. Not like you perhaps. Is that it? Or not like I should be.

SIMON. Okay, look, no, I know where this is going.

HANNAH. Simon.

STEPHEN. Gentlemen…

PAUL. No, no I do not want to disagree, Stephen. I want to agree. But I am not afraid to argue to agree.

HANNAH. Paul

PAUL. It is wrong.

HANNAH. Paul, off the record. (*A tiny nod to* MICHAEL.)

PAUL. I do not have an 'off the record'.

SIMON. Okay   TOM. (Just a broken one)

PAUL. We are here to make
a decision.*
                              MATTHEW. (*'Clarify,'
                              really)

HANNAH. I feel strongly, personally – my personal opinion like you is important to me, of course it is. But I'm trying to argue for perspective. Above and beyond. There are many, many ways to look at this, I know, but from where I sit – at home, but also here, all of us, looking out over the provinces if you will – I think it's undeniable that there's at least one simple truth: and that is that things have changed. 'Times are changing.'

PAUL. Yes, I agree with that.

SIMON. (Good)

MATTHEW. (That's true)

HANNAH. That is the central issue.

PAUL. I disagree*

HANNAH. You do?

JAMES. (*Yes)

TOM. (Really?)

JOHN. (So do I)

PAUL. Yes. It is the catalyst
for *a* central issue.

MATTHEW. I think that's
semantics

SIMON. Okay

PAUL. Not at all, Matthew.

Do we give in? Do we
follow? Do we stay
strong?

MATTHEW. (Well, I don't
know maybe not)

SIMON. We're not 'giving
in.'

STEPHEN. Let's avoid
certain provocative phrases
for now, Paul.

PAUL. Do we allow ourselves to be changed?

HANNAH. Do we evolve, remain current? And the answer is
yes, that's what I'm saying, yes we do, we do. We evolve. In
simple terms that's our challenge, Paul – don't you think? –
in all of this. How do we remain current as well as truthful.

PAUL. It is not.

HANNAH. Sorry?

SIMON. (Does he just say no to everything?)

STEPHEN. Simon.

PAUL. You are saying that we – me, the people I represent,
John represents perhaps, James – we are not current. That is
what you are saying, is it not?

HANNAH. No

TOM. (No)

PAUL. We are backward.

HANNAH. Wait, no, I haven't said that or inferred, not for an instant

PAUL. We represent a very large constituency. They are, I assure you, very much of this same current world you are 'looking out over' from here. They feel strongly.

HANNAH. I understand that, Paul, I'm not trying to –

PAUL. In fact they feel that currently a lot of people are trying to irrevocably change the organisation they joined, that they currently belong to, they currently support. So, Hannah, you talk about being current –

HANNAH. Please don't misrepresent what –

PAUL. But are you *being* current? This talk?
This is a kind of dictatorship.

TOM. What?!	SIMON. What?!
DANIEL. (Paul, um)	MATTHEW. That's a little
STEPHEN. Paul	

PAUL. Dictatorship. Not leading – but dragging. Kicking and screaming if necessary. Applying medicine 'for their own good'. Like the death penalty.

MATTHEW. Death penalty?!	HANNAH. I'm sorry?
DANIEL. WHAT?	JAMES. Colonialism
STEPHEN. (Daniel)	TOM. Hold on a second
	JOHN (*to* MICHAEL). (Don't write this down, please)

PAUL. Ask the people, ask them if they believe in the death penalty. They do. Every survey. But more and more places are stopping it. Why? Is it because they don't listen to the people? Is that what you are proposing?

HANNAH. Of course not.

PAUL. Well listen to our people then. Here we are. We feel strongly.

Pause.

HANNAH. 'My people' don't believe in capital punishment.

PAUL. Pardon?

HANNAH. Just so you know. So if you asked them –

PAUL. It is an example.

HANNAH. If you asked them they'd say no. It's illegal, / in my state. And we believe

JAMES. (Immoral, perhaps? In your culture?)

PAUL. Things are very different where you are.

HANNAH. Yes.

STEPHEN. Exactly. Yes.
Things are very different where we all are.

Some mumbles of agreement.

But this organisation represents difference, or the scope of difference we can embrace together. You see, it can literally be many things to many people. And if we take ourselves as a group, a group of leaders who – obviously faced with very different circumstances – share a set of core beliefs, goals… The question is how do we best represent all of those goals, those beliefs. We need each other to stay strong, to keep the organisation strong. We can always do more together.

JOHN. Why would anyone join an organisation he didn't like?

Pause.

MATTHEW. Who do you mean, John?

JOHN. 'One.' Anyone.

SIMON. Perhaps they like most of the things in it. Not all of the things.

TOM. (Or people)

JOHN. Stephen, for instance.

Pause.

Who wants us to change.

STEPHEN. I am responsible for allowing us all to change, John.

JOHN. Same thing.

HANNAH. It's completely different.

JOHN. Open too many doors and you get nothing but cold wind rushing round inside the house.

STEPHEN. If we don't agree we don't exist, John. At a certain level, that's all. I'm not on one side or the other.

PAUL. How can that be?

Little pause.

STEPHEN. I have to stand in front of everyone at the same time. I have to look them all in the eye.

Pause.

We can still consider other approaches

MATTHEW. (I understand, Stephen, but…)

JOHN. Stephen…

JAMES. No

TOM. (Don't say 'steering committee'.)

STEPHEN. A report. Recommendations, / a three-month trial…

HANNAH. Please don't give up

SIMON. (I don't think so)

TOM. (I need to get out of here)

JOHN. I made a promise

PAUL. If someone walks away and someone stays who gets the name – assuming the name is the stakes. Hmm?

No response.

It is not such an easy question is it?

It used to be simple. Now your people are not so interested
in what you have to say – what any of us have to say, I know.
But the people where I come from, they are very interested.
They feel strongly about everything we say. They demand
strong leaders. So. We talk about change. And yes, a very
great deal has changed. You are right. But change is so difficult to control. It sneaks up on you. It is a rolling snowball,
even in this heat. Which of you is going to say 'we will *not*
change'?

No response.

You see, everyone is afraid because you have been accused
of taking a stand all too often. Centuries. You overcompen-
sate. We on the other hand have always taken a stand but
usually been ignored. Our provinces have not had the power
to make our stand much more than a little knee-bend in your
eyes. Like we were only ever warming up for the race, yes?
But now when we stand it is clear. We are very tall. It takes a
long time to count us because there are so many.

So I ask you: do you want to stand together or opposed?
Because it is up to you. We are already standing.

Pause.

We cannot save everyone, my friends. We cannot run after
them. What we can do is build a place for people to visit. Not
a literal place – we can do that too, that is what bingo is for,
isn't it, Hannah? The Church Bazaar – (we are expanding
our buildings here in Africa every year, of course) – but I am
talking about a place built with ideas. We can build a haven
with ideas that anyone can come to if he wants. But if we
make that promise, my friends – 'we promise you this haven
will be solid, strong, a refuge' – we cannot constantly rebuild
it. We cannot paint it a different colour every season because
of fashion. The man we want to help will not find it. He will
not be helped. We may think we've only changed a little bit,
but if he cannot find us and recognise us, he will not be
saved.

A knock at the door.

I am only pointing out that the colour I stand for is the colour
this building has always been painted.

A knock at the door.

JAMES. What's that?

TOM. The door.

MATTHEW. Is there someone out there?

TOM. Of course there's someone out there.

SIMON. What do they want?

JOHN. They're interrupting.

Little pause.

MICHAEL. (Coffee.)

JOHN. What?

DANIEL. Coffee. It's the coffee. Room service.

MATTHEW. The coffee

HANNAH. Of course it is

STEPHEN. Coffee has arrived

PAUL. (No)

TOM. Thank God

MATTHEW. (Tom, please)

JAMES. Coffee.

Little pause.

MATTHEW. Who's going to get it?

No one moves. MICHAEL *looks inquisitively to* DANIEL
who shakes his head slightly.

STEPHEN. I'll go.

He moves towards the door.

PAUL. We are supposed to be sequestered.

STEPHEN. What?

JOHN. No contact. Until we have decided.

MATTHEW. ('Clarified')   SIMON. (Everything by the
                                                book)

PAUL. Close your eyes.

DANIEL. Paul

STEPHEN. No, it's fine.
    I will close my eyes. We'll all close our eyes.

TOM. Oh come on

STEPHEN. Until we've decided.
    We all close our eyes.

    Through the door.

    Hello?

JOSEPH (*off*). Hello.

STEPHEN. Who's there?

JOSEPH. It is the porter.

STEPHEN. Ah.
    Coffee?

JOSEPH. Joseph.
    Yes.

STEPHEN. Yes. You have the coffee?

JOSEPH. Yes sir; I have coffee and I have tea.

STEPHEN. Excellent. Good.
    (*To the others*.) Eyes.

    *All close their eyes which remain shut throughout the fol-
    lowing.* STEPHEN *opens the door.* JOSEPH *in the doorway
    with trolley.*

    Hello.

JOSEPH. Hello.

STEPHEN. You have the coffee.

JOSEPH. Shall I give you the tray?

STEPHEN. Is it very heavy?

JOSEPH. It is pretty heavy, yes. I have a trolley.

STEPHEN. Okay, well. Maybe, then… shall I just help you, or…

JOSEPH. Why don't I come in and set it on the table. Then you can help yourselves. People like that.

STEPHEN. Yes, thank you.

JOSEPH does so, carefully laying out the different coffees, teacups, teapot, water, etc., stealing glances at the group, all of whom remain seated with eyes shut. He finishes. Silence.

Have you gone?

JOSEPH. No. I am still here.

STEPHEN. Good

JOSEPH. The coffee is on the table.

STEPHEN. Thank you very much.

JOSEPH. Thank you.

STEPHEN. There's – did you see? There's money on the table.

JOSEPH. This is courtesy of the hotel, sir.

STEPHEN. Well, thank you.

JOSEPH. You are welcome.

STEPHEN. But – for you, for – I don't know how much… perhaps you can take what you think…

Little pause.

You must think this is very odd.

PAUL. What are you talking about over there, Stephen?

JOSEPH. No

STEPHEN. I'm just thanking the waiter.
  (*To* JOSEPH.) We've made strict rules.

JOSEPH. They told me you were a special group.

STEPHEN. I don't know about that.

JOSEPH. Can you do something for me?

STEPHEN (*beat*). I can try.

JOSEPH. Will you tell the hotel the service was good. My boss.
  I was helpful

STEPHEN. Oh

PAUL. Stephen?

JOSEPH. If I was helpful.

STEPHEN. Yes. Of course. You were. You have been.

JOSEPH. He does not like me.

STEPHEN. I'm sure that's not true.

JOSEPH. It is.

STEPHEN. Well. I'll tell him, yes

PAUL. What are you talking about?

JOSEPH. He hates me.

STEPHEN. No, I don't think so.

JOSEPH. If you looked at me, maybe you could tell.

STEPHEN. Yes. I mean, no I don't think so.
  I would look at you, of course, but.
  We're trying to make a decision.

JOSEPH. I see.

STEPHEN. You're not injured or something?

JOSEPH. Forget it. It is okay.

STEPHEN. I'm sure it will be fine. With your boss. I'm sure. Thank you, very much.

PAUL. Why does he not like you?

Little pause.

My friend? Are you still there?

JOSEPH. Yes.

PAUL. Tell me your name.

JOSEPH. Joseph.

PAUL. Why does your boss not like you, Joseph?

JOSEPH. I don't know.

PAUL. You are good strong African man?

JOSEPH. I hope so.

PAUL. You work hard for your wife, your children.

JOSEPH. I do not have a wife.

PAUL. Your girlfriend.

JOSEPH. I live with my mother. My aunt. My sisters

PAUL. You are the man of the house.

JOSEPH. Yes.

PAUL. You believe in God?

JOSEPH. Of course.

PAUL. And you go to church?
Or perhaps you go to a mosque, you can tell us, we are very tolerant.

JOSEPH. I go to church, sir.

PAUL. Good.

JOHN. Very good.   JAMES. Yes

PAUL. What church do you go to, Joseph?

SIMON. You don't have to   TOM. (Paul)
    say.

JOSEPH. The Holy Mountain of Fire Mission to the World.

PAUL. Ah, yes, I know it. Of course I have seen it on TV

JAMES. Yes

PAUL. James knows it. It is impressive

JOSEPH. Yes

PAUL. Outside the city; in the old football stadium.

JOSEPH. Yes

PAUL. My colleagues probably do not know this big church.

SIMON. No   HANNAH. I don't think so

MATTHEW. I don't think so   TOM. No

STEPHEN. Paul

PAUL. Perhaps you can tell them, Joseph, what it is like. What
    is special about this church.

    JOSEPH *is silent. Looking at them.*

STEPHEN. I'm sure Joseph has to get back to work.

PAUL. It is very popular, isn't it, Joseph? People go weekday
    evenings, as well as Sundays, right? Hundreds.

JOHN. More. Thousands.   JOSEPH. Yes.
                                On some days.

PAUL. They finish their work, they go home, and they wash
    themselves and put on their suits, right? Their best dress.
    Everyone washes their car and puts on hats and fine clothes.
    They get in their cars and they drive out the highway to the
    stadium. A very dangerous road, Joseph, is it not?

JOSEPH. Yes

PAUL. There are attacks.

JOSEPH. There are bandits. And holes; a lot of accidents.

PAUL. And attacks.

JOSEPH. Sometimes.

PAUL. From non-believers, is that not right? Attacks from those
who do not believe?

Little pause; no response.

And counter-attacks, people fighting back.	JOHN. (You know who he means)

JOSEPH. People have defended themselves. Sometimes.

PAUL. Of course they have. In my parish too. Joseph, parish-
ioners of mine have been attacked in their own homes,
imagine that, while they are sleeping in their own beds. And
they have defended themselves; they have defended themselves and their beliefs for what is right against hatred. And
some have died martyrs. But we are strong, aren't we?

And when everyone drives on that highway together there
are no attacks, are there?
Your pastors, Joseph, they know how to win. Not geography:
Evangelism. Numbers.
So what do they say to you? When you get in there, in that
big stadium, what do they say to you about God?

Pause. JOSEPH *looks at them all.*

JOSEPH. They say we must ask from God what we want.
He wants us to have it.
And He shows us. Like our ministers have so many nice
things blessed by God: cars, and clothes, and houses –
But first we must be pure, and clean.
We must raise up the church, give to the Holy God to
receive, and God will give back to us a hundred times again.

MICHAEL *has opened his eyes, looking at* JOSEPH.

God will enter the spirit into us and make us iron-strong
Protect us from all the disease and evil corruption and
hunger

And from the bullets and the violence and from accidents
And from evil spirits and witches.
And He will bring us everything we need and we ask for.
We must demand it.

Silence.
JOSEPH *sees* MICHAEL, *eyes open – stares.*

PAUL. Thank you, Joseph.

STEPHEN. Yes. Thank you, Joseph, for the coffee, thank you
very much.

Thank yous from all.

PAUL. We will tell your boss you are a good man. A good
worker. And we will pray for you.

JOSEPH. Thank you.

He glances at the money on the table.
MICHAEL *closes his eyes.*

JOSEPH *leaves the money, exits.*
Silence.
Slowly the group begin to open their eyes.

STEPHEN. Well.

Eventually TOM *moves to get a coffee, followed by*
MATTHEW – *they're interrupted:*

PAUL. You see friends…?

SIMON. Paul   MATTHEW. Please.

STEPHEN. Paul.   TOM. (Not now)

PAUL. We are not the only ones offering God

STEPHEN. Of course

PAUL. But this is Christianity without suffering, Christ without
the cross, it breaks my heart, but you see: people here *want*
God. Here where we live there is still pestilence and plagues,
evil emperors, corruption – demons for some. When we look
to the Bible we do not see 'stories' like you. We see truth.

We do not need interpretations – we need strength.

SIMON. We're not just talking about interpretations

PAUL. We are not embarrassed of what we read

HANNAH. We're not embar-   TOM. (I really need a coffee)
rassed

PAUL. 'We are bringing you this book: the Truth,' that is what
you first say. Now you are saying, 'We want it back'.

STEPHEN. No   DANIEL. No

SIMON. That's not true   MATTHEW. I don't think so

PAUL. 'This is how you must read it.'

HANNAH. We want to *share* it, Paul

PAUL. When you come here with your ideas it is always
'peace', 'assistance'. If we come to you it is 'interference'.

STEPHEN. Please   HANNAH. No, Paul. No

PAUL. Perhaps you need our mission now, but you still want to
talk about 'culture'.

SIMON. *You* talk about culture. / You talk about fighting*

PAUL. Yes, we have our   JAMES. (*You are naive)
culture you do not under-
stand   SIMON. (Really)^

MATTHEW. Well…   JAMES. (Yes, to the
                                dangers. Blind)
JOHN. (^Yes)

PAUL. But we do not cast the first stone, Simon. No. We have
challenges too, of course. For example: we have struggled
with polygamy. Many men take several wives, and when
their fathers die, their brothers, they must also take their
wives – this is a cultural tradition. It is very difficult to con-
vince people, but we have disallowed it. We must, you see: it
goes against the Bible.

We know it is not easy to follow God.

MATTHEW. (There's actually quite a lot of polygamy in the Bible)

TOM. (Yes)

HANNAH. Please don't throw us to the lions, Stephen.

Pause.

STEPHEN. No one is being thrown to the lions.

HANNAH. We are. You are.

STEPHEN. Me?

HANNAH. We represent millions too.

PAUL. Of course

JAMES. (Not nearly as many million)

HANNAH. They don't sing in the choir, perhaps. They don't necessarily come to our buildings week in week out, but they know we're their foundation and they count on us. In their hearts. Absolutely; I truly believe that.
Everyday laypeople – like Michael here, maybe – / we have a responsibility to these people too.

MATTHEW. (Michael?)

TOM. (Michael?)

MICHAEL. (Oh)

DANIEL. (Sorry, Michael.)

SIMON (*nodding to* MICHAEL). Him.

MATTHEW. (Surely he goes to church regularly ^ – he's a committed volunteer, isn't he?

JOHN. Cultural Christians, Hannah?*

DANIEL. (^Yes. Of course he does)

PAUL. *This is a very difficult constituency.

HANNAH. But it's also a tradition

JAMES. For you.

HANNAH. And we listen, we listen to everyone. (*To* STEPHEN.) *You* count on us to listen, Stephen, to be understanding

STEPHEN. Everyone is listening

HANNAH. You know we'll be the ones to bend over backwards and accommodate, compromise, back down even

STEPHEN. No

HANNAH. You know we're not going to get out the machetes

Silence.

STEPHEN. (Hannah. No.)

PAUL. Yes. I see.

SIMON. No

JAMES. Machetes

TOM. (Oh no…)

JOHN. This is outrageous, Stephen.

MATTHEW. Hannah

STEPHEN. No

DANIEL. (Oh no)

PAUL. This is unacceptable

HANNAH. I'm sorry.

STEPHEN. This rhetoric, these words. From everyone.

MATTHEW. (It isn't right)

It has to stop

HANNAH. It's a metaphor. That's all

It must stop.

He constantly uses metaphor

HANNAH. Well it's up to you, Stephen, isn't it?

Pause. Everyone's attention.

STEPHEN (*quietly*). And what do you think I should do?

Make a declaration?
'This is what I believe, follow me,' regardless of the consequences?
Then I can simply sleep easy, come what may; wash my hands?
Everyone wants me to condemn.
Do you think that will change anyone's mind? Or his heart?

We can only find an agreement together.

SIMON. We're not going to agree

STEPHEN. But we're still talking, don't you see?
We're more than the sum of our parts because we aim to
discover and emulate God's way. In that alone we can be an
example. We can be a model here on earth how human
relations might be.

HANNAH. I remember when we met, Stephen.

STEPHEN. Hannah, please don't

HANNAH. Students. We stormed the barricades for change.

STEPHEN. Don't be sentimental, we're not students now

HANNAH. That was an example, too.

Pause.

PAUL. It is very hot. But I think the coffee is going to go cold.

He smiles.

A break is in order.

Then we can talk all night about what is right, what is wrong,
the memories of our youth, I do not mind.

And then we will vote.

Pause.

STEPHEN. Coffee.

Blackout.

2

MICHAEL *and* JOSEPH *in a hotel room.*

MICHAEL. Do you want anything? A water, maybe? Sparkling water from the minibar.

JOSEPH. How about you bring me home?

MICHAEL. What? You mean to your?

JOSEPH. With you.

Little laugh, both.

MICHAEL. Okay

JOSEPH. Okay

MICHAEL. Of course

JOSEPH. Okay, like Helen of Troy.

MICHAEL. Sorry, like?

JOSEPH. It is not Helen of Troy?

MICHAEL. I don't know what you're talking about.

JOSEPH. She is Greek.

MICHAEL. No, I know who Helen of Troy is

JOSEPH. Brought home as a prize after war.

MICHAEL. I don't think that's Helen of Troy.

JOSEPH. I am sorry, I thought

MICHAEL. No.

JOSEPH. But I am thinking of a Greek story

MICHAEL. Maybe

JOSEPH. Spoils after

MICHAEL. I don't know

JOSEPH. That is not the word?

MICHAEL. I don't know, I don't know the story. You're thinking of, I mean.

JOSEPH. Yes. I think I am probably wrong.

MICHAEL. Yes.

Pause.

JOSEPH. It is okay.

MICHAEL. Pardon?

JOSEPH. It is okay.

MICHAEL. Oh. Yes, of course.

JOSEPH. It is not okay, Mark?

MICHAEL. No, no of course it is.

JOSEPH. Good.

MICHAEL. Yes.

JOSEPH. 'Joseph.'

MICHAEL. Sorry?
    Ah, 'Joseph', yes, I haven't forgotten.

JOSEPH. We are just tired.

MICHAEL. We're just chatting, yes.

JOSEPH. Yes.

Pause.

MICHAEL. I'm going to…

He gets himself a water from the minibar.

JOSEPH. Do you want to have a shower?

MICHAEL. Sorry?

JOSEPH (*scratching his chest in imitation of* MICHAEL). You would like to wash.

MICHAEL. No. It's just.

JOSEPH. I can wait.

MICHAEL. It's okay.
I can have a bath later.

JOSEPH. What is wrong?

MICHAEL. Nothing.

JOSEPH. So you can have a shower, it is okay.

He imitates MICHAEL *scratching his chest again.*

MICHAEL. Sorry, it's just

JOSEPH. I know

MICHAEL. I've, all over my

JOSEPH. My cum

MICHAEL. Chest well, yes, but it doesn't matter whose, it's just

JOSEPH. But it is mine

MICHAEL. Yes, but

JOSEPH. It smells

MICHAEL. No, yes but

JOSEPH. Terrible

MICHAEL. It always

JOSEPH. So it is okay

MICHAEL. Yes. Yes, it's fine. It's absolutely fine. Thank you.

JOSEPH. You can take a shower.

Little pause.

What do you think will happen?

MICHAEL. Nothing.

Little pause.

But. I do have to get ready.

JOSEPH. You have never been with an African boy.

Little pause.

MICHAEL. I don't really like to talk about. After. Okay?

JOSEPH. 'Joseph.'

MICHAEL .Yes, Joseph, okay?

JOSEPH. We are only chatting.

MICHAEL. Right, well, that's what I'm saying, I suppose.
Usually. I don't, really. Usually.

JOSEPH. What do you usually do?

MICHAEL. Nothing. That's just it, there is no.
Nothing.

JOSEPH. I am the only one.

Pause.

MICHAEL. I think you should probably go now.

JOSEPH. Yes. Okay.

MICHAEL. Thank you. Really. Joseph.

JOSEPH. Yes.

MICHAEL. Okay.

Pause.

JOSEPH. Maybe I am sick.

MICHAEL. What?

JOSEPH. Many African boys get sick

MICHAEL. No

JOSEPH. They do

MICHAEL. No wait

JOSEPH. Yes

MICHAEL. You're, you said I *asked* you said

JOSEPH. Yes

MICHAEL. We were careful

JOSEPH. But you got it on

MICHAEL. No

JOSEPH. Yes my

MICHAEL. Yes but, no so what, no the problem's not

JOSEPH. No

MICHAEL. No come on

JOSEPH. Yes

MICHAEL. Listen

JOSEPH. Okay

MICHAEL. No listen, Joseph listen to me

JOSEPH. You must have wondered?

MICHAEL. Well, I asked

JOSEPH. Yes

MICHAEL. Yes and you said

JOSEPH. You trusted me

MICHAEL. That's right, I trusted you, that's exactly it.

JOSEPH. And we were careful

MICHAEL. Yes yes

JOSEPH. Yes

MICHAEL. Yes because for both of us we were careful, right? Because.

We have an understanding.
Don't we.

JOSEPH. I could have lied.

MICHAEL. This isn't funny, Joseph

JOSEPH. Or I slipped it off

MICHAEL. Joseph – Jesus – look, I mean, this is

JOSEPH. African men do not like condoms

MICHAEL. I've heard that

JOSEPH. It is for pussies

MICHAEL. Joseph

JOSEPH. Even the bum-fuckers think it is for pussies

MICHAEL. Stop it right now, Joseph. Stop it.

JOSEPH. I am not sick. Like that.

Little pause.

I feel bad.

Little pause.

MICHAEL. Right. Well.
Good.
Not, but.

You don't need to feel bad.

Anyway. You're fine, right?

JOSEPH. I am not sick, Mark.

MICHAEL. I know.

JOSEPH. What do you think will happen if you have a shower?

Pause.

MICHAEL. It's time for you to go.

JOSEPH. I might steal something.

MICHAEL. No. That's not what I think.

JOSEPH. But you want me to go.

MICHAEL. Yes, I do. I do want you to go. You have to go. Thank you. I have to check out.

JOSEPH. I am a porter. I go into rooms all the time.

MICHAEL. I know

JOSEPH. What would I take

MICHAEL. I don't think

JOSEPH. What do you have that is so special from all the other guests in the hotel?

MICHAEL. Nothing.

Little pause.

JOSEPH. I think this is a funny situation. You are very far away from home, Mark. But also I am far away from home, even though I come in these rooms every day – (*Laughs.*) – no, not cum, I do not mean.
I am sorry, my English is not very good. I cannot explain. But maybe you see. I am far away from home now too. We are friends, but we are both alone. I think our homes are very different where we live.

MICHAEL. Joseph. I tried to be very clear before we. When. I think your English is very good.

JOSEPH. Thank you.

MICHAEL. You're welcome.

JOSEPH. I do not think so

MICHAEL. No it is, and I think you understand.

JOSEPH. This has never happened to me.

MICHAEL. Well, no.
No.
It's never happened to me either, Joseph.

JOSEPH. Really?

Little pause.

MICHAEL. I'm asking you to leave.

JOSEPH. What do you think the General's wife said when he came back with Helen?

MICHAEL. I want you to go now please

JOSEPH. I think it would be very hard for most women

MICHAEL. I don't think Paris had a wife when he kidnapped her but in any case

JOSEPH. You know the story?

MICHAEL. I have an idea

JOSEPH. I am wrong

MICHAEL. You're confused, yes

JOSEPH. But I imagine if he *did* have a wife it would be very very difficult to explain to this wife at home what had happened.

Pause.

MICHAEL. Probably.

JOSEPH. He returns to his beautiful palace with a young prize. Spoils. She follows him. This is the Greek story I was thinking of. The wife is not happy, probably. But maybe the General says to the wife, But you see, wife, I am helping this friend as well as you. She needs my help, just like you need my help. This does not mean I do not love you, but look how she needs help. Look how much love I have to give.

MICHAEL. Are you threatening me?

JOSEPH. No, please. Of course I am not.

MICHAEL. Okay

JOSEPH. I respect you.

MICHAEL. Fine.

JOSEPH. I do not want to hurt you.

MICHAEL. Well. No. Good.

JOSEPH. I know you are good.

MICHAEL. Yes. Right.

JOSEPH. I think your wife is probably good.

MICHAEL. Don't

JOSEPH. I am sorry but

MICHAEL. No

JOSEPH. Maybe you have children

MICHAEL. Stop it

JOSEPH. Or your neighbours

MICHAEL. It's none of your business no

JOSEPH. But I think all of you must try to live a good life,
Mark

MICHAEL. It's none of your business

JOSEPH. Just like here. Here we are good here too

MICHAEL. I'm sure you are

JOSEPH. Yes we are good in our neighbourhoods too, but it is
very hard

MICHAEL. Yes I know, I know that, Joseph. *I know*.

JOSEPH. Yes, of course you know.

Little pause.

MICHAEL. No.
I'm sorry.
I mean, I understand.
I know that I'm
Lucky.
That

My 'neighbours' as you say that
It's mostly an accident of birth, isn't it?
That's why it's so important for me to meet people like you,
Joseph.
I respect you too.

JOSEPH. We are unlucky here

MICHAEL. Yes

JOSEPH. But also I am lucky, like you: I have this job.
  It is a very nice hotel.

MICHAEL. It is.

JOSEPH. And the service is very good, don't you think?

MICHAEL (*beat*). Are you taking the piss out of me?

JOSEPH. No.

MICHAEL. Is that what this is about?

JOSEPH. No

MICHAEL. Because I'm losing my patience with this

JOSEPH. I see England every day

MICHAEL. Yes, splendid

JOSEPH. And America

MICHAEL. Tourists

JOSEPH. On TV

MICHAEL. Right

JOSEPH. Beautiful

MICHAEL. Well it's TV isn't it

JOSEPH. And it is only ten hours on a plane from here, is that
  true?

MICHAEL. What? England? Yes, England's ten hours and a bit,
  yes

JOSEPH. I want you to take me to England with you.

Pause.

MICHAEL. You're joking.

JOSEPH. I am not joking.

MICHAEL. That's ridiculous. I can't.
    You know I can't.

JOSEPH. I know people who have gone there.

MICHAEL. I'm sure you do.

JOSEPH. Usually they do not go on planes. They hide in the
    back of trucks, they go on boats, they die in the ocean

MICHAEL. Okay

JOSEPH. It takes longer than ten hours.

Little pause.

MICHAEL. You're a smart young man, Joseph.

JOSEPH. Yes.

MICHAEL. You know this isn't how the world works.

JOSEPH. I know. It is circumstances, that is what I say too.
    It is not your fault.

MICHAEL. No.

JOSEPH. It could be anyone, but it is you.
    You are here now.
    Now you can see how you can help.

MICHAEL. Can I?

JOSEPH. Yes.

MICHAEL. How? Help how, do what, do?
    Pack you in my bag?
    Buy you a ticket beside me on the plane and lead you home
    to dinner?
    Come on, Joseph. Give me a break.

And you need
Passports, visas, skills, all of that, do you have?
Okay, yes, yes you probably do, because you're smart
You've studied you do probably, okay, well.
Do you know what will happen?
You'll end up a cleaner.
You'll end up mopping floors, picking fruit or something
Half the people who come they're disillusioned, you know
that right,
They're miserable, trust me, they regret it.
It isn't TV.

JOSEPH. No

MICHAEL. No, so, I can't help you. I'm sorry. I'm very sorry.
So.
I'm going to go for a little walk, Joseph, and when I'm back
you'll be –
Okay?
We're going to forget this, Joseph.
When I get back you'll just be gone. End of story.

JOSEPH. No

MICHAEL. Yes you will

JOSEPH. This is my only chance

MICHAEL. This is like those trucks, don't you see that?

JOSEPH. No it is nothing like

MICHAEL. You can't get to England like this. This isn't the
way, you can't

JOSEPH. What is the way?

MICHAEL. Well, I don't know, I don't know the way you
apply
You go through the channels that's what I said,
You fill out

JOSEPH. This takes too long

MICHAEL. Probably, it probably does but

JOSEPH. It is impossible

MICHAEL. Well then what can I do? That's what I'm saying:
    What do you really expect me to do?

JOSEPH. Invite me.

MICHAEL. What?

JOSEPH. Maybe this would help.
    I can say: 'It is okay, they want me.
    I have the correct papers. I have a job.'
    You can tell them you want me to come.
    That I must come. That it is important.

MICHAEL. That's what you want me to do?
    Administrative?
    Find the right forms or.
    To bring you over

JOSEPH. Okay

MICHAEL. Okay, well.
    That's different.
    That's.
    It's actually a good idea, Joseph. We can do that.
    So. Why all the macho – ?
    It doesn't matter

JOSEPH. No

MICHAEL. No, okay, look. Good. This is what we're going to
    do then. Together. To start with I can give you my details,
    and you can give me your email, phone, address if you have
    all that, and what I'll do is some research

JOSEPH. Research

MICHAEL. Yes, I'm going to
    I'll look into what needs to be done, the first step, and we
    can go from there. I'll find out what we need to know, what
    we do and I'll let you know.
    I'll call you.

(*Looking for his wallet*.) And here, I'm going to give you a little… Where's…? I want to give you something…

JOSEPH. I have your wallet.

Pause.

MICHAEL. Right.

JOSEPH. And your passport.

Silence.

MICHAEL. I see.

Pause.

JOSEPH. Your name is Michael.

Pause.

MICHAEL. Yes.

JOSEPH. Mark is short for Michael in England?

MICHAEL. No, of course it's not.

JOSEPH. What should I call you?

MICHAEL (*beat*). Michael.
    Mike.

JOSEPH. Mike.

MICHAEL. It doesn't matter

JOSEPH. It must matter.

MICHAEL. Give them to me please.

JOSEPH. Maybe this is not your room.

MICHAEL. It is my room give me my things, please.

JOSEPH. My full name is Joseph. No one ever calls me Joe. It is important.

MICHAEL. Look. Joseph.
    I'm sorry.

This is very difficult, I know, for.
I mean both of us.
I'm.
I don't have any power, with this, any of this anything just to
You understand?
I'm just a volunteer. There are dozens of us here, this is a big
conference, they picked me out for the meeting last night but
I'm doing administrative
Name-ticking not.
I run a small business, at home.
We make envelopes. But.
It's very small, I don't have any money.
This is volunteer work, my church
And –
I wanted, and my – my wife wanted me more involved and
there was a list you could sign up and I just wanted to get
away for a bit
From things, but –
And also because I wanted to see Africa
Come over here, of course,
I've always wanted to see Africa, always.
And this was an incredible opportunity and I thought –
Well we do a lot of work, our congregation, we're connected
'Twinned' it's called, to a sister church here and we send
money but
It's always appealed to me, Joseph
Africa.
Even when I was a boy.
The picture books and films and
The space.
The heat.
The mystery of it, the Jungle.
The secret sort of dark
Beauty

Look.
I'm not good at this.
I'm, usually.
I don't.

I made a mistake, Joseph. I don't know what I'm doing. I'm
married.
I'm going home today.
Please.
Give me my wallet and passport back, please.

JOSEPH (*going through wallet*). So many numbers.

MICHAEL. Yes

JOSEPH. I am a number also: 'One of many.'

MICHAEL. Take the cards

JOSEPH. What?

MICHAEL. You can have the cards if you want

JOSEPH. I am not stupid

MICHAEL. Of course not

JOSEPH. You will cancel them

MICHAEL. I won't

JOSEPH. In ten seconds

MICHAEL. No

JOSEPH. Why are you treating me like

MICHAEL. I'm not treating you

JOSEPH. I do not want your credit cards

MICHAEL. Well what do you want then?

JOSEPH. I want what you have.
    That is what I want.

MICHAEL. Well you can't. I'm sorry.
    That's the truth.
    Isn't it?
    I wish it weren't, but.
    I'm not the government. I'm not the whole world. I'm just a
    man.

So. There it is. Now we're two men standing in a hotel room.
What are we going to do?
I want my passport back. What do you want?

JOSEPH. You can have the wallet

MICHAEL. I don't care about the wallet I want the passport

JOSEPH. I want God to punish us.

MICHAEL. What?

JOSEPH. Do you think He will?

MICHAEL. No.
I have no idea.

JOSEPH. I do not think so because He is not watching, is He?
That is why you worship him.

MICHAEL. He is, Joseph.
He is watching.

JOSEPH. What does He see?

MICHAEL. He sees a young man who is very angry. And He
understands.

JOSEPH. I mean when He looks at you, Mike.

MICHAEL (*beat*). He forgives me.
I hope.

JOSEPH. I want a god who sees everything.
The god who punished Sodom and Gomorrah, who saved
Noah and the animals two by two. The same rules for
everyone. Not a god who makes us live in purgatory.

MICHAEL. The Crowne Plaza Hotel is hardly purgatory.

JOSEPH. Do not make fun of me.

MICHAEL. It's not even
The Crowne Plaza isn't really even your country, Joseph, do
you realise that?!
This – do you? So don't

Don't lecture me.
Step outside. What do you think the punishment is outside
the Crowne Plaza for

JOSEPH. For what?

MICHAEL. For unlawful confinement, for blackmail

JOSEPH. For fucking boys

MICHAEL. No

JOSEPH. Fucking African boys

MICHAEL. No.
Okay, yes then
Okay, *yes*.
For fucking, for men fucking men, what do you think they'll
do

JOSEPH. I fucked you

MICHAEL. The details aren't important

JOSEPH. It matters

MICHAEL. What do you think they'll do because

JOSEPH. It is illegal

MICHAEL. Yes, I know exactly, if

JOSEPH. What you are is illegal

MICHAEL. No. No.
No. If I have to tell them, Joseph, go to my Embassy
If I have to. I will.
I will.
I'll tell them.
If I have to.
That you fucked me.

Against my will, maybe.

JOSEPH. They will kill us.

MICHAEL. No they won't

JOSEPH. Yes. They will break my legs, they will whip me

MICHAEL. Don't try to frighten me

JOSEPH. When my family hear / they will kill me

MICHAEL. No. No, this is sick, get out of my room.

JOSEPH. No

MICHAEL. Get the fuck out of my room! Get out!

JOSEPH. No

MICHAEL. Get out! Get the fuck out of my way! Get out now!

They struggle.

JOSEPH. Apana a ha miye sita énda sita énda uko kirofa Sita
   ina fana uni sayidiye Ni sayidiye miye Ni sayidiye miye
   weyé uko kirofa weyé *weyé*!

   MICHAEL *is thrown violently to the floor.*
   Silence.

MICHAEL. Who is this helping, Joseph?
   Not you.
   Please.
   This is suicide.

   JOSEPH *spits on him.*

   Little pause.

   MICHAEL *wipes his face.*

JOSEPH. I am a soldier.

MICHAEL. What?

JOSEPH. It surprises you because you are the victim.

MICHAEL. Stay away from me.

JOSEPH. When soldiers come running out of the trenches
   maybe it seems like suicide.

MICHAEL. No

JOSEPH. This is how an army wins a war.

MICHAEL. We can get you to England, Joseph.

JOSEPH. They just keep coming.

They just keep coming and you fight them and you shoot them but they keep throwing themselves at you. Those black faces keep coming until you cannot focus any more and fight any more and you get tired but they keep coming and coming because they have no choice. They cannot go back. Maybe it is the shit in the trench or the big generals controlling the war, but their only hope is to run straight ahead and keep shooting because eventually one of them will have to make it. The rest will follow him.

There is a knock at the door.

They freeze.

A second knock.

Who is that?

Neither move.
Another knock.

MICHAEL *laughs nervously.*

DANIEL (*off*). Michael?

Pause.

Michael?

MICHAEL. Yes?

JOSEPH. No.

DANIEL (*off*). Michael?

MICHAEL. Tuck your shirt in.

JOSEPH. Wait.

MICHAEL. Straighten your tie.

JOSEPH. No.

They stare at one another a moment. MICHAEL rises, opens the door.

DANIEL. Ah

MICHAEL. Daniel

DANIEL. I thought maybe you were still asleep, or checked out

MICHAEL. No. Sorry, I didn't hear you.

DANIEL. They'll all be down soon.

MICHAEL. I'm sorry, I'm just about ready.

DANIEL. I can wait in reception, I just

MICHAEL. No, I'm almost, I'm just about ready.
I lost my passport.

DANIEL. Oh dear.

MICHAEL. No, I found it again. This young chap did. Joseph.

DANIEL. Ah, brilliant. Well done, Joseph.

MICHAEL moves to JOSEPH. *He retrieves the passport from him.*

MICHAEL. Thank you.
I've got to…

He disappears into the bathroom.
DANIEL *stares at* JOSEPH.
Sound of items being quickly collected.

(*Off.*) I'm just grabbing my… one second…

Pause.

DANIEL (*to* JOSEPH). How are you?

JOSEPH. Very good.

MICHAEL reappears with shaving kit – throws it and scattered items into a bag. Continues to pack quickly.

MICHAEL. Here we go.

DANIEL. It's been a horrible night.

MICHAEL. Oh?

DANIEL. We've just finished

MICHAEL. Really?

DANIEL. Not finished. Stopped. There's no agreement.

MICHAEL. Really

DANIEL. After you were 'released', yes, it got worse

MICHAEL. Really

DANIEL. It looked like the end there for a moment or two. We all should have left to be honest.

MICHAEL. Right.

DANIEL. Anyway. I need you.

MICHAEL. Okay.

DANIEL. Breakfast has become a contest: who's eating in which dining room

MICHAEL. Politics

DANIEL. Etiquette

MICHAEL. Of course, yes. / I'm just about ready

DANIEL. It's silly, but we do need to make a push. We need the numbers

MICHAEL. At your table

DANIEL. 'A show of strength.'

MICHAEL. I understand

DANIEL. I'm sorry.

MICHAEL. Please. Ready.

DANIEL. No, all the volunteers have been a godsend this week and I know you're supposed to be administrative, you're supposed to be officially 'off-duty'.

MICHAEL. Daniel

DANIEL. It's almost over

MICHAEL. It's my privilege. Really.

DANIEL. Thank you.
I also want to remind you that
All that, last night, what was said on both sides

MICHAEL. It was a private meeting. Of course.

DANIEL. Thank you.
Okay. Shall we – perhaps the bags can be brought down

MICHAEL. It's fine

DANIEL. Don't be foolish.

He motions to JOSEPH.

Please; young man.

JOSEPH *reaches for the luggage*.

MICHAEL. Get your hands off!

Pause.

It's fine.
I can

DANIEL. (Oh)

MICHAEL. It's fine

DANIEL. Sorry

MICHAEL. No, sorry

DANIEL. I'm sorry

MICHAEL. I'm a man I can manage perfectly, it's okay, sorry.
Thank you.

DANIEL. Right.

MICHAEL. I'm sorry.

DANIEL. No.

MICHAEL. It's

DANIEL. No, it's fine. It's fine. But, please let me

MICHAEL. I'm okay

DANIEL (*taking a bag*). Really, I've got it.

MICHAEL. Thank you. Sorry

DANIEL. 'Many hands.'

MICHAEL. Thank you.

DANIEL. We're down in the second dining room again

MICHAEL. Good

DANIEL. It will probably be okay. But as I say, 'the numbers'

MICHAEL. Just say the word.

DANIEL. Thank you.

   They exit.

   JOSEPH *is left alone*.

3

MICHAEL *and* SHELLY *at home*. MICHAEL *holds a Bible*.

SHELLY. I thought they were birds

MICHAEL. They're not birds

SHELLY. No but I thought they were
    I read that sparrows

MICHAEL. Well they're not

SHELLY. And pigeons could actually

MICHAEL. Which are actually rats

SHELLY. Sparrows though
    and other birds
    could get into the soffits.

MICHAEL. Exactly.

SHELLY. But

MICHAEL. That's exactly it

SHELLY. No, that it wasn't such a big deal, Michael.

MICHAEL. No?

SHELLY. Some people actually encourage them.

MICHAEL. But they're not sparrows.

SHELLY. I know.

MICHAEL. So.

SHELLY. We thought they were

MICHAEL. I said squirrels

SHELLY. You said rats

MICHAEL. Or squirrels

SHELLY. Or rats. Okay. Well. Squirrels.
Good for you.

MICHAEL. Thank you.

Little pause.

SHELLY (*indicating the Bible*). Why don't you put that down.

MICHAEL *looks at her. Puts Bible down*.

You're sweating.

MICHAEL. I'm not sweating.

SHELLY. Okay.

MICHAEL. I'm not sweating.
I was reading.

SHELLY. Yes.

She stares at him.

MICHAEL. Yes.

Little pause.

You really can't hear that?

SHELLY. How are they getting in, Michael?

MICHAEL. I have no idea.

SHELLY. I thought you looked?

MICHAEL. Of course I looked, you've seen me, I've looked all
over

SHELLY. Okay

MICHAEL. I've *stood* out there for ages

SHELLY. I know

MICHAEL. Well

SHELLY. Looking up at the sky. Staring into space.

Little pause.

MICHAEL. Did I?

SHELLY. Into the heavens.

She imitates him. Little pause.

MICHAEL. Well, I have no idea how they're getting in.
But we have to get rid of them.

SHELLY. I won't kill them.

MICHAEL. I'm not going to ask you to kill them. But

SHELLY. No

MICHAEL. Well, no, but. There is a problem

SHELLY. I'm not going to have them killed.

MICHAEL. There's a problem because it's illegal, Shelly.

SHELLY. What's illegal? / Saving them?

MICHAEL. Against the rules, some rules, releasing them.
You're not allowed to trap squirrels and then let them go.

SHELLY. It's illegal to let them live?

MICHAEL. Essentially. Yes, I suppose.

SHELLY. That's ludicrous. Whose rules?

MICHAEL. Well, technically they're 'pests'

SHELLY. It's cruel

MICHAEL. They become psychologically scarred.

SHELLY. What?

MICHAEL. Really. From the traps. That's what I'm told.
I mean, think about it, if they're stuck in the traps, say the
trap goes off while you're at work

SHELLY. Or while you're at work.

MICHAEL. Yes, while either of us are at work

SHELLY. Because we both work

MICHAEL. I know we both work.

SHELLY. We're a double-income family, aren't we?

MICHAEL. Yes

SHELLY. Couple.
Or if you're at a Bible retreat.

Pause. He stares a moment.

MICHAEL. What I mean is if *one* isn't around, it goes off, you
don't know, the squirrel's trapped in there for hours.

SHELLY. God

MICHAEL. It panics. It's going mad it can't get out

SHELLY. Ew

MICHAEL. Yes, it's not very nice. It's released into the wild.
It's.
Distressed

SHELLY. That's terrible

MICHAEL. Damaged, yes. I'm just telling you what I found.

SHELLY. But killing them

MICHAEL. What they say is that *when* you release them, if we
did, you can't just put them in the garden because in two
seconds they're back in your loft. They'll eat through anything to get back in

SHELLY. Anything?

MICHAEL. Once they've made a home – yes – they're driven.
The most
More determined than rats, anything
So they have to be taken somewhere else, by someone.

SHELLY. The country.

MICHAEL. Yes. Like into the country. That's right.

SHELLY. Okay.

MICHAEL. Okay.
    Oh, no, we can't do it

SHELLY. Why not?

MICHAEL. They come back, they've been known to
    Fifteen miles, twenty miles, the same place

SHELLY. Twenty miles?

MICHAEL. We can't drive out into the country five, six times
    every time we catch a squirrel

SHELLY. Why six times?

MICHAEL. Why are you giving me such a hard time, Shelly?!

SHELLY. Six?

MICHAEL. Well four.
    We've got – (it's an infestation)
    I've seen at least four squirrels up there.

SHELLY. When did you start reading the Bible?

MICHAEL. What?

SHELLY. The Bible.

MICHAEL. I've always read the Bible.

SHELLY. At home. Not that I'm aware of.
    I mean, you may be reading it other places, of course

MICHAEL. Like at church?

    Little laugh, both.

SHELLY. Yes, I suppose. I *have* seen you at church

MICHAEL. Busted

SHELLY. Unless you've been doing it in secret. At home. Other
    places.

MICHAEL. It's a vice, you're right.

SHELLY. No, I know.

MICHAEL. It's not that odd, Shelly, is it? We go to church, we're in church groups

SHELLY. You're going on retreat again.

MICHAEL. Not again. It's the first time.

SHELLY. Africa

MICHEAL. Africa wasn't a retreat

SHELLY. Well

MICHAEL. You used to say 'get more involved'

SHELLY. Within reason

MICHAEL. Am I being unreasonable?

SHELLY. Before Africa you never used to go to Bible study.

MICHAEL. At our church.

SHELLY. Our church doesn't have Bible study.

MICHAEL. Well, that's where I go

SHELLY. To the *building* – with the happy-clappers

MICHAEL. What?

SHELLY. The happy-clappers who rent the building in the week.

MICHAEL. That's not what I call them.

SHELLY. Are you becoming an Evangelist, Michael?

MICHAEL. What? Becoming – ? (*Little laugh*.) No, I'm reading the Bible a little more seriously

SHELLY. With Evangelists

MICHAEL. With Christians.

SHELLY. On weekdays

MICHAEL. Okay

SHELLY. Sunday isn't enough?

MICHAEL. I've always read the Bible, Shelly. I find it
comforting.
I'm finding it – very comforting, I guess, re-reading. It gives
me strength.
But maybe I'm embarrassed

SHELLY. Really?

MICHAEL. Of people's reactions. Yes.

SHELLY. Me? Now?

MICHAEL. I don't know: people's reactions like your reaction.

SHELLY. I'm sorry.

Little pause.

The thing is
You don't look comforted.

MICHAEL. No?

SHELLY. You look distracted

MICHAEL. Really?

SHELLY. On edge, yes. Since you've been back.
From Africa.
Like you have to concentrate on being you.
Nervous.

MICHAEL. We have squirrels in our attic.

SHELLY. I mean generally, all the time

MICHAEL. They're in there all the time.

SHELLY. That's why you need comfort?

MICHAEL. Everyone needs comfort, Shelly

SHELLY. Even squirrels.

Silence.

MICHAEL. The people I spoke to said they can't just drop
them off either, that's the big problem.

They're territorial
And if you drop them at a park or something and the others
already there, the squirrel family in the park or what-have-
you they block them out and they won't survive even if you
want them to.

SHELLY. They're a family up there?

MICHAEL. I don't know.

SHELLY. You said

MICHAEL. Someone I spoke to suggested
Apparently they live in families, four or five, six sometimes

SHELLY. Parents and babies, you mean?

MICHAEL. I don't know. They kick the father out

SHELLY. Really?

MICHAEL. Apparently. I don't know. Around birth

SHELLY. Nature.

MICHAEL. Yes. What I mean is they can't just instantly
acclimatise to a new park.

Don't look at me like that.

SHELLY. You are so cold, Michael.

Little pause.

MICHAEL. What?

SHELLY. Black and white like this. Taking it out on squirrels.

MICHAEL. Taking what out?

SHELLY. I don't know: what? You tell me. On me. Why you're
so angry.

MICHAEL. I'm not angry. I'm trying to make a point

SHELLY. Why you need comforting

MICHAEL. What?

SHELLY. You're sweating

MICHAEL. I'm not sweating

SHELLY. You're always sweating

MICHAEL. Why do you keep saying that, I'm not sweating

SHELLY. If you're not sweating you're praying.

MICHAEL. What's wrong with – ?
Maybe I'm sweating because we have these
This dangerous plague in our attic, Shelly, they can chew through electrical wire and
Since when is our religion, Shel
Looking to Jesus to try to find some sense of understanding and
Comfort, yes, and blessing for God's forgiveness – and for strength, for purpose –
For something with a little more balls than Farley's wishy-washy Sunday service why should I feel *guilty* about that? Why do I have to feel guilty?

SHELLY. Forgiveness for what?

Silence.

MICHAEL. Do you want to come on the Bible retreat?

SHELLY. For not paying attention?

MICHAEL. What?

SHELLY. Not counting. You're not counting, are you? Days. You're not going to ask.

Pause.

I got my period.

MICHAEL. What?

SHELLY. I mean blood.
In my mucus.
My period has started. Or will start.

MICHAEL. I'm sorry.

Little pause.

SHELLY. Squirrels

MICHAEL. I know

SHELLY. Are you?

MICHAEL. What?

SHELLY. Sorry? Or happy?

MICHAEL. Happy?

SHELLY. Relieved.

MICHAEL. No.

SHELLY. At the end of the day are you? At the end of the month relieved? Because sometimes some people you can tell the way they look what they want and what they don't want.

MICHAEL. You think I'm lying to you?

SHELLY. I'm thirty-nine.

MICHAEL. I'm forty-two.

SHELLY. This is the most important thing in the world to me and it's not working.

MICHAEL. You don't know that

SHELLY. I do know that, it isn't working – is it? And your plan is to wait and leave it till it takes care of itself.

MICHAEL. I've been tested.

SHELLY. I've been tested.

MICHAEL. Yes, well I've been tested and it was

SHELLY. Abnormal

MICHAEL. Slightly, / once

SHELLY. Your sperm were

MICHAEL. The morphology

SHELLY. Deformed

MICHAEL. Irregular

SHELLY. *Yes*

MICHAEL. *Yes* exactly *irregular* which
A very small percentage sometimes
Which is not necessarily permanent or even a barrier or unusual

SHELLY. No

MICHAEL. No so what I'm saying is the doctors you know they did
The doctors said it doesn't mean we can't conceive naturally
All other things being equal

SHELLY. Naturally

MICHAEL. Yes, so
Yes
I have, I *have* tried to do something
I've done – I am doing something, I'm doing something
Every bloody month I go through, I

I don't have hot baths.

SHELLY. Every month what?

MICHAEL. Why do you want to make me feel bad?

SHELLY. You think for me it's a passionate whirlwind? It doesn't feel a touch mechanical?

MICHAEL. It's stressful, we both know

SHELLY. Lie back and think of England

MICHAEL. I understood what you meant the first time.

SHELLY. So we're trying? Three little pokes a month?

MICHAEL. Well. I'm not sure what else we can do.

SHELLY. Yes you are.
    You are.
    I want to have a baby more than anything in the world.
    And you don't.

    Or you won't.

    Pause.

MICHAEL. For me the issue is a little more.

    She looks at him with disdain.

    What? It doesn't matter because you've decided?

SHELLY. We've decided, we talked about

MICHAEL. Trying

SHELLY. And we've tried everything

MICHAEL. That's what I'm saying

SHELLY. Except IVF. We've tried everything but IVF, Michael.
    That's the next step, isn't it? The last step.

    Pause.

    So what?

    Little pause.

MICHAEL. For me IVF is a bit

SHELLY. What?

MICHAEL. I find it.
    I'm not sure I agree with it.

    Pause.

SHELLY. Agree?

MICHAEL. Yes.
    I know it sounds, to you it sounds.
    Odd.

SHELLY. It does rather, yes, what's there to *agree* with

MICHAEL. Well

SHELLY. You never said this before

MICHAEL. Philosophically we talked

SHELLY. Disagree with what?

MICHAEL. Well

SHELLY. Giving us a chance to have what we want?

MICHAEL. No, the whole.
    No that's not it, it's.
    It seems sort of
    There are questions, for me
    There are.
    The numbers.
    For instance what they do with the extra embryos and
    Or the hormones the drugs, will we suddenly have
    Triplets or quintuplets or sextuplets or

SHELLY. When did you start believing this?

MICHAEL. And it's very
    Clinical. And.
    We're Christians, Shelly.

    Little pause.

SHELLY. What?

MICHAEL. There are religious questions.
    For me. Moral questions.

    Life is a gift.
    It's not necessarily –

    There are so many people suffering, population

SHELLY. You don't think it's natural?

MICHAEL. I didn't say

SHELLY. Modern science

MICHAEL. No

SHELLY. The child will be something, what, a freak or?

MICHAEL. No not the child.

SHELLY. *Us*, we'll?

MICHAEL. The process is
No I know the science

SHELLY. I'm a woman, Michael

MICHAEL. Yes I know, exactly.

SHELLY. What?

MICHAEL. There are for me a lot of questions about
The process.
There are no guarantees.

SHELLY. What the fuck do you know about natural, Michael?

Staying up all night watching TV.
Going away.
(*The Bible*.) Reading.
Sweating.

Pause. She stares.

MICHAEL. They make mistakes, you know.
People end up with the wrong child.

SHELLY. Being *Christian*?

MICHAEL. Yes.

SHELLY. Do you think God hates women?

MICHAEL. Of course not.

SHELLY. I would do anything in the world to have a child,
Michael. Anything.

Otherwise, what is the point?

Silence.

I deserve this.

MICHAEL. It's important to count our blessings as well
     What we've already been given

She stares.

     I've been to a lot of places, Shel

SHELLY. Don't

MICHAEL. Well. I've seen people who can't even eat, children

SHELLY. Because you've been to Africa?

MICHAEL. I'm just saying it's not a right.

SHELLY. You would deny me a child?

MICHAEL. I'm not denying you anything.
     You're my wife.

SHELLY. What's wrong with you?

MICHAEL (*picking up the Bible*). Look I'm.
     Nothing's wrong with me, Shelly
     Nothing, but
     We don't know everything.
     All we do know is God has a different path for each of us
     and maybe God makes these things so difficult for a reason –
     Because he's testing us, and we have to figure out what he
     wants us to do and what he wants us to be and.
     How to be strong, Shelly.

SHELLY. God wants me to have a child, Michael.
     As a woman. I know he does.

     Why would God hate us?

He looks at her. Silence.

Doorbell, offstage.

     Who's that?

MICHAEL. I have no idea.

SHELLY. Were you expecting someone?

MICHAEL. No.

Little pause.

The pest control.

SHELLY. What?

MICHAEL. The guy to

SHELLY. But.
I thought we were talking about

MICHAEL. We are talking about

SHELLY. Well how come he's here?

MICHAEL. I'm doing something about the problem, Shelly. It's a serious problem.

SHELLY. I see.

MICHAEL. I still want to talk to you about

SHELLY. Yes?

MICHAEL. Seriously about. I asked them about releasing the squirrels.

SHELLY. Did you?

MICHAEL. Yes, because I knew it would bother you

SHELLY. I thought it bothered you?

MICHAEL. Yes I *knew* it bothered me I *thought* it would bother you so

SHELLY. So

MICHAEL. So I spoke to them.

SHELLY. And they said it's illegal.

MICHAEL. It is illegal, yes, but they could.
Or they can.

SHELLY. Really.

MICHAEL. Yes.
It's quite a bit more expensive. But they can. For extra.

SHELLY. And so you said yes.

MICHAEL. Well, I said I wanted to talk to you. Obviously.

SHELLY. Okay.

MICHAEL. So. We're talking.

SHELLY. And I said I don't want them killed if we can help it.

MICHAEL. So. I can tell him that we want them to catch them, take them away and release them no matter what.

SHELLY. Yes.

A knock at the door, offstage.

Into the country.

MICHAEL *moves to answer the door.*

Together. As a family.

MICHAEL. Together in the country.

SHELLY. Somewhere beautiful.

MICHAEL. Right. Okay.

SHELLY. Good.
Do you think they really will?

MICHAEL. What?

SHELLY. Take them into the country and release them?

MICHAEL. That's what we're paying them for, the park or something

His mobile phone rings.

SHELLY. I know but

MICHAEL. So I assume

SHELLY. Do you?

MICHAEL (*answering phone*). Yeah? No
We're here, we're in. I'll just come round to the front now
I'll be right there.

SHELLY. Or do you think they'll just drive off with them in the
   back then.
   Turn the corner.
   And.

Little pause.

MICHAEL. I don't know.

SHELLY. No.

Pause.

MICHAEL. I'm going to let him in.

SHELLY. I think it's sinister.

MICHAEL. Do you?

SHELLY. Yes.

MICHAEL. Well.

SHELLY. I've made an appointment. To see a consultant.
   (*Holding a business card.*) I've got his name right here.

 MICHAEL. Right.

They stare at one another.

Light knock at the door.

SHELLY (*indicating the Bible*). Put that down.

Neither move.

4

Meeting room/lunch room at MICHAEL*'s envelope manufacturing company.*

A mass of samples laid out (perhaps on table) in blocks of red envelopes, white envelopes, and thin, multicoloured envelopes.

Two very large pictures/posters of skyscapes (sun breaking through clouds) adorn the walls.

MICHAEL *in a suit.*

HARRY. This is a little embarrassing, Michael.

MICHAEL. There's no need to be embarrassed

HARRY. No

MICHAEL. I'm listening

HARRY. It's just that
    Some of us

    No offence

MICHAEL. Okay

HARRY. In different ways I suppose we're a little
    Uncomfortable.

    Little pause.

MICHAEL. Right

HARRY. We're a little uncomfortable with
    Some of the direction of things

MICHAEL. Direction

ALISON. (Tone)   DAVE. ('Policies')

HARRY. Approach, maybe

MICHAEL. You don't mean the donation envelopes here?*

BILL. *No. / No.

His phone rings.

DAVE. (Yes)

Because these are just my suggestions, you under-stand, amid everyone else's suggestions –

HARRY. *Well, they're part of it, yes

He cancels the call.

ALISON. But they're all manufactured already, right?

They're just samples I picked up, ordered online –

MICHAEL. Yes, but I think we could do it better, Alison. (*Picking up samples*.) Look: they're usually distributed in packs of fifty-two, one for each Sunday of the year with an extra twelve for once-a-month donations, then seasonal holi-days, birthdays: that's a lot of envelopes if you get an entire congregation – that's a full-blown opportunity

HARRY. Depending on the size of the congregation.

DAVE (*reading envelope*). 'The New Testament word Grace is not an excuse for my giving little rather than much.' (*Another envelope*.) 'For the Pastor's Birthday.' (*Another*.) 'For the Pastor's Anniversary.'

Pause.

MICHAEL. I'm saying there's a market. We don't have to agree with every word. We're talking about challenges to our industry: the decline of traditional postal service, expanding what the envelope can be. (*Indicating envelopes*.) There's an 'extra-postal' demand here, if you will.

ALISON. It's a bit 'niche', though, isn't it, Michael?

MICHAEL. No, I don't think so, Alison, I'm surprised to hear you say that. I think it's specialised. I think it's exactly the kind of thing that's right for us and our culture here, absolutely. I'm certain of it.

Pause.
MICHAEL*'s phone rings again.*
He checks the caller again and deliberately turns it off.

HARRY. That's kind of it, Michael.

MICHAEL. What? You disagree

HARRY. What do you mean by 'our culture here'?

Little pause.

MICHAEL. Well.
Okay, Dave's red envelopes, the Chinese envelopes
What kind of tradition are the red envelopes, Dave?

DAVE. It's kind of feng shui, I suppose

MICHAEL. But is that Buddhist or Confucian or? What is it?

DAVE. When you put furniture in particular / places so

MICHAEL. No, I know what feng shui is, but I mean

DAVE. You mean religion. What religion?

MICHAEL. No.
No, tradition, culture; I mean:
What comes from who we are together in this building;
Where we come from, how we work, what we share, what
we like.

For instance –
In days gone by you're all aware this used to be a printer's
shop –
The cloakroom now, they used to have a small chapel
attached to the factory back there, didn't they

Some nods, reluctant 'yeses'.

And all the printers, all the machinists would put down their
tools twice a week for a half-hour service together. They
brought their families on Sundays. The point being – not the
religion – but there is a history to this place, a little lost
maybe, but it's here, and last Sunday at church when I saw

the donation envelopes for the umpteenth-millionth time I
suddenly just thought: Aha, *yes* the envelope industry faces a
challenge, but it's a challenge that has been *set* for us, and
there's an answer already offered, a tradition here, and it fits
– a ready market offered to us that fits with the building and
the people and our company –

DAVE. People are uncomfortable here, Michael.

Silence.
MICHAEL *looks at the group.*

MICHAEL. Well. I don't want anyone to be uncomfortable.
Obviously.

Little pause.

HARRY. Some of the guys on the floor, for instance. Aren't
they, Bill?

BILL. Some of them are a little
Annoyed, I suppose, yeah

MICHAEL. Are they?

BILL. Well not

MICHAEL. 'Annoyed'?

BILL. Concerned

MICHAEL. Okay. About?

DAVE. About the pictures, for example.

MICHAEL (*indicating the 'cloud' pictures*). The new pictures?
These?

BILL. The old pictures

MICHAEL. Old pictures?

HARRY. (Come on, / Michael)

BILL. Well the shop-floor pictures, their pictures in the shop,
yeah.

MICHAEL. I was concerned about the old pictures in the shop

HARRY. Sure, but   DAVE. (Obviously)

MICHAEL. Alison must have been concerned, Bill

DAVE. (Alison never com-   BILL. Alison / doesn't work
    plained   in the shop

                                    ALISON. (I can look after
                                        myself)

MICHAEL. I mean they were of girls with their tits hanging out
    (sorry Alison) weren't they?

BILL. Some of them

MICHAEL. Yes some breasts hanging out, not exactly con-
    ducive to work, or / working or

HARRY. (Our culture)

MICHAEL. Yes Harry, that's exactly what I mean, not very
    family-friendly or what-have-you

DAVE. There are no families working here

MICHAEL. Client-friendly, visitors. 'Morally' friendly. You
    know what I mean. You're not suggesting they were appro-
    priate, are you?

Little pause.

Speak up.

HARRY. I think maybe the problem is the way they were taken
    down, Michael.

Little pause.

MICHAEL. Right

HARRY. I think some people feel kind of
    Curtailed.

MICHAEL. I'm running a business here.

HARRY. There's an atmos-   BILL. (Of course)
    phere

MICHAEL. Did I step on their rights? / Their freedom of
expression?

HARRY. Come on

MICHAEL. No one's forced
to work here*

ALISON. Michael, we're
trying to explain

DAVE. Not everyone '*likes*'
the same pictures

BILL. But it's not just pictures

DAVE. *What?

BILL. There is an atmosphere

DAVE (*indicating the posters*). For instance I don't like these
new pictures of God everywhere.

MICHAEL (*beat*). These aren't pictures of God, Dave. They're
clouds.

DAVE. Okay, well, they *suggest* God, / don't they?

MICHAEL. That's your interpretation, I suppose, / but

HARRY. Michael

MICHAEL. I'm sorry, / but is this a witch hunt?

ALISON. No one's attacking you, Michael – no!

HARRY. Of course it's not   BILL. No

DAVE. (Christ)

MICHAEL. Well that's very good, / thank you

HARRY. We're trying to talk about changes

MICHAEL. But we're talking about me, aren't we?

Silence.

ALISON. We're worried about you, Michael.

Pause.

MICHAEL. Well, you don't need to worry about me, thank you.

Pause. MICHAEL looks at them.

He chuckles slightly.

Look.
I'm sorry. I do understand.

Part of this is the name, isn't it? You see changes – there
have been changes, yes – changes in approach or decisions
made maybe in what you think of as 'Christian' and that
makes you uncomfortable –

DAVE. Yes   BILL. (A little, yeah)

MICHAEL. Which we should probably just call 'good business
practice' but

HARRY. Well, no

MICHAEL. But I do understand. Then I bring the envelopes.

He smiles.

Forget the envelopes.

He looks to the group.

I don't want to make anyone uncomfortable. I want to be
honest.

It's always been important for me to work from my princi-
ples of faith. And maybe I'm trying harder than ever, but I
don't want to force that on anyone. Absolutely not.
What's difficult to explain is – and I'm going to be perfectly
honest, here –
When you have a personal experience of God
It clears the waters.
The murky water is suddenly clean, and you can see through
to the bottom, or the surface, you know, the whole sky. The
muck is gone. Indecision.
And when you discover His strength, and you start to share
something of that iron will, feel it yourself, in your own will,
and when you experience that God is alive everywhere you
want to share it and the way you do is by *being* alive, and
being vibrant and full of His strength and leadership, and
that honestly gives you a kind of

Well, clarity – to make decisions, see – to see what to do

DAVE. But it's making you schizophrenic, Michael.

Silence.

MICHAEL. Is it?

DAVE. We don't know who we're going to run into from one moment to the next.

Some days it's Michael Matey – smiles, full of compassion, as likely to give you a hug as a bollocking. 'Take a long lunch if you're stressed.' A bit moralistic maybe, but / kind

ALISON. (Dave)

DAVE. Other days it's Michael Money. And he's all bottom-line, tight deadlines, numbers. He's a taskmaster, a control freak, a cut-throat. No hugs. He wants to know why you're so slow and incompetent.

We don't know where we are, Michael. Because we don't know who you are.

Silence.

MICHAEL. And what do you think I should do about it?

No reply.

Alison? You're a fellow Christian.

Pause.

ALISON. I don't know.

Pause.

It would only be a personal opinion.

MICHAEL. That's what I'm asking for.

Little pause.

ALISON. Well.
I think you need to listen to both these Michaels.

Then, I think you need to take one of them, drag him into the cellar – and kill him. And if you can't kill him, you need to

chain him up and not let him out so that the other Michael
might be able to breathe. You might relax.

Silence.

She shrugs.

I don't know.

Little pause.

MICHAEL. No.
I don't think you're right, Alison. No offence

ALISON. (It's just my opinion.)

MICHAEL. God reconciles.

ALISON. Maybe

MICHAEL. A single deity sends His only son both human and
godhead to be killed on earth and live for ever? And the mir-
acles – the dead made living, the water wine, the stone water.
The five loaves and two fishes, and the merchant cured of
leprosy – how else can we interpret that? 'God wants us to
walk in the shoes of our faith and wear our best business
suit'; I read that somewhere, and I believe it. He wants to
reconcile the contradictions in our life, that's what I believe.
God reconciles. He must. He does.

Silence.
He looks at the group.

Little laugh.

But, like I say – maybe I'm trying too hard.

HARRY. Mike

ALISON. (Michael)

MICHAEL. So. Dave.

DAVE. Michael.

MICHAEL. Your suggestion is the red Chinese envelopes: we
should look to the Chinese market.

SHELLY, *finely dressed in a long coat, high heels, smart dress, steps into the open doorway, unnoticed.*

DAVE. It's okay, Mike, really

HARRY. Why don't we take a break?

BILL. Yes   ALISON. That's a good idea

MICHAEL. No, no, it's fine, I want to hear more about these ideas. Dave is right: there's a market there too. There are billions of Chinese. (We're not in China, / but okay)

ALISON. (Michael)

MICHAEL. You said they're like shields, right Dave? Fending off negative energy

DAVE. I don't want to be patronised, Mike

MICHAEL. No they're blessings, too, you said, that's interesting. Tell us how that works. Please.

Little pause. DAVE *looks to the others.*

DAVE. Well.
They're lucky. Red is for luck. People give them to their children with money in them and pray they don't get old, for one thing

ALISON. What? / Why?   MICHAEL. That's interesting

DAVE. Yeah. On New Years.   BILL. Really? That's dark

ALISON. That can't be true

SHELLY *raps lightly on the doorframe. All turn.*

HARRY. Shelly   MICHAEL. (Shel)

SHELLY. Sorry, gentlemen,   BILL. Mrs Thomas.
Alison
                                      DAVE. Alright, Shelly?

ALISON. Hello, Shelly

HARRY. It's good to see
you.
                                      BILL. You look lovely

SHELLY. I've been trying to reach you, Michael.

Little pause.

MICHAEL. Is everything alright?

SHELLY. You didn't answer.

MICHAEL. Well, we're in a meeting.

SHELLY. I need to speak to my husband. I'm sorry.

| HARRY. We can grab a coffee. | DAVE. No, no worries. |
| | BILL. Of course. |

MICHAEL. We're kind of in the middle of something, Shelly.

Little pause.

HARRY. Why don't we take a break, Michael? We need it.

Pause.

MICHAEL. Alright.

HARRY. It's good to see you, Shel.

General 'goodbyes'… all exit.
SHELLY *and* MICHAEL *stare at one another.*

MICHAEL *shuts the door.*

SHELLY. I've been calling all morning.

MICHAEL. Have you heard something from the hospital? Is something wrong?

SHELLY. No.

MICHAEL. Because you've made me look a little foolish.

SHELLY. I left a dozen messages. What are those posters?

Little pause.

MICHAEL. They're new. They're an experiment; I'm not sure it's working

SHELLY. Who's Joseph?

Silence.

MICHAEL. Sorry?

Little pause.

SHELLY. I was lying down this morning and I heard this
    Rattling first, like rippling, then this crash.
    Glass

MICHAEL. At the house?

SHELLY. My heart stopped.
    Then I heard it again outside the bedroom and I couldn't
    figure out what it was. Then I realised. Someone's throwing
    stones.

MICHAEL. What?

SHELLY. Pebbles.
    Someone throwing stones at the window

MICHAEL. This morning?

SHELLY. You go to work very early these days, Michael.

MICHAEL. There's a lot of work to be done.

SHELLY. It was still dark.
    I pulled back the curtain and I thought I could see a shadow
    moving under the elm tree. A boy.
    Then I saw him pick up more stones and wind up and I
    thought he's going to break every fucking window in the
    house and I banged on the glass and he turned and looked up
    at me – arm cocked. Just stared.
    He stood there staring and I stood there staring.

MICHAEL. In your nightgown.

SHELLY. I was dressed for work. I was up and dressed

MICHAEL. You were up?

SHELLY. I felt sick. *Nauseous*. So I lay down again.

MICHAEL. It could be the drugs. The hormones.
    Maybe it's the Serophene

SHELLY. What?

MICHAEL. The nausea.

SHELLY. His name's Joseph.

MICHAEL. Is it?

How do you know?

SHELLY. He rang the doorbell

MICHAEL. Okay

SHELLY. I went downstairs, opened it

MICHAEL. Right

SHELLY. Hello, he said.
Why are you throwing stones at my house? I said
Does Michael live here?
Did you break my window? On purpose?
Why are you throwing stones at my windows?
I must talk to Michael, he said.

You know my husband, I said, that's why you're throwing
stones?

He thought my name was Helen.

MICHAEL. Really.

SHELLY. I am sorry, Helen, I must speak to Mike.
I got so angry.

MICHAEL. Right

SHELLY. Why don't you tell me what you have to say, why
don't you tell me why you're throwing stones at my house?
I cannot. I must speak to Mike. It is important.
And I slammed the door in his face.

Little pause.

MICHAEL. I can understand that.

SHELLY. Can you?

MICHAEL. You must have been scared.

SHELLY. It sounded like a threat.

> (*Little laugh.*) I've never shut the door on anyone before
> Not even salespeople
> Not even Jehovah's Witnesses.
> My heart was going.

MICHAEL. You were angry

SHELLY. I was scared.
> I just felt so. Bad.

MICHAEL. And then he went?

SHELLY. He stood there. He didn't knock, or throw more
stones or even sit down. He just stood there.

MICHAEL. What did you do?

SHELLY. I opened the door again
> Invited him in

MICHAEL. Did you.

SHELLY. That's when I saw how awful he looked.

MICHAEL. Sick?

SHELLY. Poor.

> I made tea and sandwiches.

> Do you know what kind?

MICHAEL. No.

SHELLY. Cucumber.

MICHAEL. Really

SHELLY. I don't know why.

MICHAEL. You never make cucumber sandwiches

SHELLY. No. I know.
> I don't, do I?

MICHAEL. No. It's not like you.

SHELLY. This strange black boy sitting on our step. Eating sandwiches.

Little pause.

Who is he, Michael?

Pause.

MICHAEL. What did he say?

Little pause.

SHELLY. He said he met you when you were in Africa.

MICHAEL. Did he

SHELLY. Yes. At the hotel.
You said, look me up when you're in England and that's what he was doing this morning

MICHAEL. Is he still there?

SHELLY. What?

MICHAEL. At the house.

SHELLY. No, of course not

MICHAEL. Okay

SHELLY. Of course he's not still there

MICHAEL. I thought maybe you offered

SHELLY. I don't know who he is, Michael.

Silence.

MICHAEL. I met him while I was in Africa, Shelly.

SHELLY. 'Joseph.'

MICHAEL. I suppose

SHELLY. You suppose?

MICHAEL. Well I haven't seen him, have I?

SHELLY. You think he's an impostor?

MICHAEL. No

SHELLY. He says he's your 'friend Joseph', he knows you.

MICHAEL. I met him in Africa, at the hotel, that's true.
He's rather an extraordinary young man, actually
Very clever

SHELLY. Yes

MICHAEL. Yes, it's clear, isn't it, it's obvious

SHELLY. I don't know. I hardly spoke to him.

MICHAEL. Well.
Neither did I, really.

SHELLY. Really?

MICHAEL. Yes.
We chatted, of course, we talked
A few times about things but

SHELLY. He was staying there?

MICHAEL. He was working.

SHELLY. Really?

MICHAEL. Yes.

SHELLY. What did he do?

MICHAEL (*beat*). He was a porter.
Is a porter

He carries bags and stuff

SHELLY. I know what a porter does.

MICHAEL. Of course you do.
He asked me to help him.

SHELLY. And did you?

MICHAEL. No.
I said I couldn't.

SHELLY. Why?

MICHAEL. Well there's lots of reasons, aren't there?

SHELLY. But what did you tell him?

MICHAEL. I just told him I couldn't, Shelly. Could I?
I told him we lived in different worlds.
I tried to discourage him from coming.

SHELLY. It didn't work.

MICHAEL. No. Apparently not. No.

To be honest
In the end I felt a little 'used'.

SHELLY. Used?

MICHAEL. Yes. 'Marked', like I was a mug.

SHELLY. But you weren't a mug.

MICHAEL. I am a mug. I am. Yes.
I can understand he's probably furious with me

SHELLY. I don't believe you.

Pause.

I'm furious with you.

MICHAEL. You don't believe me.

SHELLY. I don't believe anything you say.
Anything we say. Who cares what we say any more
Blah blah blah blah.

MICHAEL. Maybe.

SHELLY. I saw his eyes.

MICHAEL. What do you mean?

SHELLY. Burning. Or seething, perhaps

MICHAEL. I don't know

SHELLY. Beautiful eyes

MICHAEL. Yes, maybe

SHELLY. Maybe *he* believed something you said.

MICHAEL. Or didn't believe something I said.

SHELLY. What did you say?

Little pause.

MICHAEL. I told him I was married to you, Shelly.
I told him I loved you.

SHELLY. Why is he harassing us?

MICHAEL. Is he?

SHELLY. Lurking in the shadows, throwing stones, ringing our
bell

MICHAEL. You gave him a sandwich

SHELLY. I wanted to help him what would you call it?

MICHAEL. Haunting.

He's like a ghost. Isn't he?
Do you see that?

He's a fury. He's like a fury, Shelly.
I wanted him to –
I tried to change the channel
You offered him a sandwich
But here he is
Do you understand?
Still furious
Staring in the windows
Do you know what I mean?
I'm just talking. But I'm trying to explain something

SHELLY. You're not just talking, no

MICHAEL. I need to explain something. I'm trying.

SHELLY. We have a child waiting for us, Michael, you know
that? In the lab, in the hospital, in a little Petri dish we have a
tiny child waiting for us. And as long as everything is

normal, they're going to put that little baby back inside me on Monday. And she, or he – whichever, because we don't care do we as long as that child is healthy, do we – he or she is going to grow and grow and then be born perfectly healthy in the eyes of God. Your flesh and blood. You're a father. Fingers crossed.

Little pause.

Fingers crossed.

MICHAEL. I hope so

SHELLY. It's not your choice. You are.

Silence.

I brought you a sandwich.

MICHAEL. What?

SHELLY. It was left over. I don't know.

And this.

She pulls out a small photograph.

He left this.

MICHAEL. What is it? / A picture?

SHELLY. There's a phone number on it, yes.

MICHAEL. You.
   It's you.

SHELLY. I thought you kept it in your wallet.
   On your person at all times.

Pause.

MICHAEL. I do.
   I didn't want to say.

SHELLY. What?

MICHAEL. Admit that I lost it.

Pause.

SHELLY. Well. It's not lost. Is it?

MICHAEL. No.

He takes the photo.
Pause.

I do love you, Shelly.

SHELLY. Then show us love, Michael.

He puts the photo in his wallet.
Looks at SHELLY.

He kisses her.
Very little reaction.
He kisses her again, more deeply.
He moves his hands to her ass.
He begins to undress her, undress himself.

She helps a little with her own clothes, but perfunctorily,
with apparent sadness. MICHAEL *becomes increasingly*
aggressive, frenetic – his effort demonstrative and fraught.

They are absolutely naked.
They struggle.

A knock at the door.

ALISON (*off*). Michael – someone's calling you.

Mike? Sorry.
There's a call for you.

MICHAEL *and* SHELLY *stare at one another.*
She is naked, still, dry.
He is naked, frozen, flaccid.

Behind them the posters like windows, or eyes.

5

A church basement. Bulletin boards decorated with children's Sunday School drawings, faded posters, etc. Double doors with glass windows, flanked with glass panels, lead to a stairway to the main church. Elsewhere, solid double doors (closed) lead to an outdoor stairwell to the car park. At the far end, a door (open) beside a (closed) banquet counter leads to a kitchen. At the opposite end a small, temporary washing line, a few articles of clothing.

STEPHEN, *in bishop's vestments.* DANIEL, *at the light switch. They both stare at –*

JOSEPH *holding a cup of steaming tea. He is shirtless. His chest is slightly scarred, his back severely so.*

Occasionally throughout, sounds of a growing assembly upstairs.

STEPHEN. Oh. We didn't know anyone was down here.
    We came down to

DANIEL. Talk

STEPHEN. Prepare. (*Holding up cards.*)
    My talk. Tweak it. Breathe.
    It's very cold.

JOSEPH. Yes

STEPHEN. You're not wearing a shirt.

JOSEPH. No.

STEPHEN. I'm sorry. We've barged in.

    Pause.

    But you're here for the scheme's launch, too, I assume? This is your church? Or you're with one of the visiting churches upstairs?

You're not press?

JOSEPH. No

STEPHEN. Well, good then. Welcome.

JOSEPH. Thank you.   DANIEL (*indicating clothes-*
                                      line). What's this?

STEPHEN. Though I should be thanking you, shouldn't I?
    That's what today is about: 'God's Buildings for All'

DANIEL. Your Grace.

STEPHEN. Daniel thinks the scheme represents weakness.

DANIEL. That's not entirely accurate

STEPHEN. This is Daniel. I'm Stephen

DANIEL. Your Grace

STEPHEN. I think it's wonderful, 'God's Buildings for All'. I'm
    happy to be here to launch it – where they're already leading
    the way. I won't be accused of 'draughty museums'. If it's
    true there aren't enough people coming through the door
    every day, I see no harm in inviting friends like you, other
    congregations, on a Tuesday or a Wednesday to use them

DANIEL. (Rent them)

STEPHEN. Daniel's afraid we could open our arms too wide.

DANIEL. I'm afraid gestures can be interpreted as defeat

STEPHEN. Public perception.

DANIEL. I'm worried people might be confused by our
    bedfellows

STEPHEN. It's lovely to be in a parish church. I don't get out to
    them enough.

    He turns to the bulletin-board drawings.

    These are exactly the same as when I was a child. They
    could be the same pictures. I miss all of this.

    He looks back to JOSEPH.

But we have barged in. And we're due upstairs, Daniel.
To welcome the masses. Speak to the press.
(*Slight smile*.) Cut the ribbon.

DANIEL looks from clothesline to JOSEPH.

DANIEL. Are you after one of these? I don't think we caught
your name. Do I know you?

JOSEPH. I do not think so.

DANIEL (*indicating* STEPHEN). Do you know who this is?

STEPHEN. It doesn't matter

DANIEL. It does matter. Do you?

JOSEPH. The white one. Please.

*Little pause. DANIEL takes down a white shirt, hands it to
JOSEPH.*

Thank you.

STEPHEN. Daniel.

DANIEL (*to* STEPHEN). No one knows who you are.

*JOSEPH puts down his tea, slowly puts on the shirt, his back
revealed to STEPHEN and DANIEL.*

They stare.

STEPHEN. I'm sorry.
Your scars.

JOSEPH. I fell down the stairs.

Little pause.

STEPHEN. Not these stairs, I hope.

JOSEPH. No.

STEPHEN. Good.

Little pause.

There are so many terrible events in the world.

JOSEPH. And people.

STEPHEN. I prefer to think people are fundamentally good, but –
Yes. People do terrible things sometimes.
We refuse to look one another in the eye, we choose poorly,
see things poorly

JOSEPH. I did not choose to fall down the stairs.

STEPHEN. No. Of course not.

Pause.

There's a wonderful window up there with extraordinary
colours. You may have seen it. Daniel doesn't like it

DANIEL. That's not true

STEPHEN. Right at the back. It's very modern, the forties,
maybe fifties – I should know this

DANIEL. It's late forties

STEPHEN. There you go: Daniel's very good with facts. In any
case, it's very interesting: very bold colours, large blocky
panels, very geometric, rather flat in appearance, I mean
intentionally. Apparently it was intended for the altar, but it
was deemed a failure. It wasn't popular at all. So they stuck
it in the back. However, what makes this window particu-
larly unusual is that, although it clearly represents Jesus
walking among the poor, unlike traditional windows it's very
difficult to determine exactly which story it illustrates. It
takes something from the Lord feeding the multitudes,
preaching the Sermon on the Mount, curing the leper, but it
still seems to be just Jesus walking among the poor. (*Little
laugh.*) 'Just'! Anyway, you understand what I mean:
'Simply'. You must look closely when you're up there,
mustn't he?

DANIEL. Yes

STEPHEN. Yes. In the one hand Jesus is holding a shepherd's
crook, or a walking stick. The other arm is stretched all the
way out. But because the image is so flat and so minimal, it's

impossible to tell if Jesus is meant to be wrapping his arms around the group walking with him – or if he's meant to be pointing the way.
It might, of course, be that one contains the other.

But the colours.
Just like when I was a boy. I only ever saw the colours.
The light coming through solid blocks of colour. That's what seemed the miracle to me then in all the windows.
The colour. Not the picture.

DANIEL *looks intently at* JOSEPH.

DANIEL. Which group are you with up there?

JOSEPH. I am waiting for someone.

DANIEL. But from which group?

JOSEPH *stares*.

JOSEPH. The Holy Mountain of Fire Mission to the World.

DANIEL. Really?

Outside the solid doors the sound of rattling – the door tested, then keys in the lock. One of the doors swings open.

MICHAEL *hurries in with plastic shopping bags. Sees everyone. Stops.*

MICHAEL. Oh. Daniel.
I

He looks to JOSEPH. *To everyone.*

DANIEL. Michael.

MICHAEL. I thought you'd be
I expected you upstairs. Hello. Welcome.

DANIEL (*to* STEPHEN). You remember Michael, from our African conference.

STEPHEN. Ah, yes, of course I do. Good evening.

MICHAEL. Your Grace.
  Hello.
  It's an honour
  Has the Reverend
  Farley –?

DANIEL (*to* JOSEPH). And this is – we didn't catch your name

STEPHEN. Yes.

MICHAEL. Good
  We know each other.
  (*To* STEPHEN *and* DANIEL.) What a pleasure.

  JOSEPH *stares at him.*

  (*To* JOSEPH.) I'm sorry I'm so late.
  (*To* STEPHEN *and* DANIEL.) I promised I'd drop him off.
  At the cinema.
  (*To* JOSEPH.) We should go.
  (*To* STEPHEN *and* DANIEL.) I'll be right back, sorry.

JOSEPH. I was about to offer everyone tea.

  Little pause.
  DANIEL *checks his watch.*

MICHAEL. Oh. Well.

STEPHEN. That's very kind, but I'm afraid we must get
  upstairs.

MICHAEL. Of course

DANIEL. I'll have a tea. Thank you.

JOSEPH. Excellent.

STEPHEN. Daniel?

MICHAEL. Right. Good.
  (*Smiling uncomfortably at* JOSEPH.) Thank you.

  JOSEPH *stares back – then moves from his place for the first
  time. Disappears into the kitchen.*

  MICHAEL *still with his shopping bags.*

STEPHEN. They're expecting us, Daniel.

MICHAEL. Yes

DANIEL (*to* MICHAEL). That's quite a badge.

MICHAEL. I'm sorry?

DANIEL. Your badge, your lapel pin

MICHAEL. Oh

DANIEL. What is it, a – / is it hands?

MICHAEL. It's hands. Yes it's hands praying.

DANIEL. Against a bible?

MICHAEL. Yes. (*Little laugh.*) It's praying hands and a bible on a shield of faith. An affectation. 'Jewellery.'

DANIEL. What's wrong with a simple cross?

MICHAEL. Nothing

STEPHEN. (Daniel)

DANIEL. We haven't lost you, too? /Already?

MICHAEL. No, no of course   STEPHEN. (It's alright)
    not

DANIEL. You're not an ardent Evangelist now

MICHAEL. No

DANIEL. A member of The Holy Mountain of Fire Mission to the World?

Little pause.

MICHAEL. No. I'm not.

DANIEL. What are you doing here, Michael?

Little pause.

MICHAEL. This is my church.

DANIEL. Of course, but the basement.

MICHAEL. I'm just dropping some things off

DANIEL. Shopping

MICHAEL. Yes

DANIEL. Groceries

MICHAEL. Some supplies, yes

DANIEL. For your friend?
Joseph?

MICHAEL (*beat*). Who?

DANIEL. Joseph.

STEPHEN. (Daniel?)

MICHAEL. His name's not Joseph.

DANIEL. Really?

MICHAEL. Yes

DANIEL. Really? I must be mistaken. I thought I recognised
him

MICHAEL. I don't think so

DANIEL. From our trip to Africa. You remember that trip?

STEPHEN. (Daniel)

MICHAEL. His name is Mark.

DANIEL. Is it?

Little pause.
He calls towards the kitchen.

'Mark'?

JOSEPH *appears in the doorway.*

JOSEPH. Can I help you?

DANIEL. Sorry. May I have two sugars, Mark. Please. If you
have them.

JOSEPH. Yes.

He disappears again.
Little pause.

MICHAEL. He's our cleaner.

DANIEL. And he lives down here?

MICHAEL. No

DANIEL. Someone's living down here

STEPHEN. Gentlemen

MICHAEL (*the clothesline, etc*.). I think this is the Sunday
   School

DANIEL. What?

MICHAEL. Doing a performance, or a project

DANIEL. This isn't a real clothesline?

STEPHEN. Daniel

DANIEL. This is a lie, Stephen. / We're being lied to

MICHAEL. (Please, Daniel.   STEPHEN. That's enough
   I'm sorry, sorry)

DANIEL. This church is in your *diocese*. There's going to be a
   press scrum / up there

STEPHEN. Stop it now, is that clear?

DANIEL (*to* MICHAEL). Are you trying to embarrass us?

MICHAEL. No

STEPHEN. Daniel!

DANIEL (*to* STEPHEN). Because this is what I'm talking
   about, Stephen: the conservatives for example have drawn
   their lines

STEPHEN. I'd rather you didn't talk, thank you

DANIEL. Because they've *decided* / you're not going to draw
   any lines of your own

STEPHEN. I'm well aware of what people are saying

DANIEL. And they're just waiting for you to wander across with something like this, / another embarrassment that plays into their hands and makes you look uncertain

STEPHEN. But I don't see the issues in terms of battle lines, do you understand that? And I'm not going to endorse one side over another

DANIEL *(to* MICHAEL*)*. Why are you doing this, Michael?

STEPHEN. Stop it! Do you hear me, stop it! Daniel.

Little pause.

Michael.

Pause.

MICHAEL. He doesn't have anywhere to go.

DANIEL. I'd like to suggest something

STEPHEN. No, Daniel

DANIEL. Why doesn't he stay at your place, Michael?

MICHAEL. That's impossible

DANIEL. Is it? / Why?

STEPHEN. Why are you so angry? Why are you turning on these men?

DANIEL. Because I'm tired, Stephen. I don't know, because if we don't set the rules I guess we have to follow what we've already got or the rules others set –

STEPHEN. What are you talking about?

DANIEL *(to* MICHAEL*)*. Why can't he just stay at your house?

MICHAEL. My wife is expecting a baby.

Little pause.

DANIEL. Really?

MICHAEL. Yes

STEPHEN. That's wonderful, Michael. / Congratulations

DANIEL. What has that got
to do with it? /Are you
converting the loft into a
nursery? Is he sensitive to
paint fumes?

MICHAEL. She has a
nervous disposition. She's
tired.
No.

STEPHEN (*to* DANIEL).
Daniel, I won't ask you
again. Are you listening to
me?

DANIEL. Some people do have rules, there are rules – for
instance: he's illegal. / If he's seeking asylum he can go
through our outreach programmes

STEPHEN. We don't know
the situation here

MICHAEL. He can't seek
asylum yet

DANIEL. Well he can't stay
here

Do you want to step
outside?

DANIEL. Sorry?

Little pause.

STEPHEN. While Michael and I talk?

DANIEL (*indicating kitchen*). I know who this is.

STEPHEN. Don't say another word, Daniel.

He's a man. First and foremost.
Who needs help.

DANIEL. We can't have a scandal here. Up there. Today. Any
day.

STEPHEN. Why would this be a scandal?
No. No, what's scandalous is

This is what we're supposed to do
In front of our eyes
Man to man
And you don't even want me to engage
To talk to him
Talk to Michael.

Pause.

STEPHEN *turns to* MICHAEL.

Michael.
Why can't Mark claim asylum?

Little pause.

MICHAEL. I don't know. Maybe he can, but he's not ready

STEPHEN. He can?

MICHAEL. It's a bit of a grey area.

STEPHEN. But he was persecuted? Was he?

MICHAEL. Yes.

STEPHEN. He was?

MICHAEL. Yes. He was persecuted.

STEPHEN. Do you know why he was persecuted?

MICHAEL. Yes.

STEPHEN. Why was he persecuted?

MICHAEL. He was sleeping with men.

Pause.

STEPHEN. I see.

MICHAEL. I don't think so.
He was sleeping with me.

Long pause.
Upstairs, the sound of people milling about now suggests a very full house.

STEPHEN. At our conference in Africa.

DANIEL. (*Exactly*)

MICHAEL. His name *is* Joseph.
I'm sorry.
He asked for my help.

JOSEPH appears in the kitchen doorway wearing a suit and tie. He carries a tray of tea and biscuits slowly to the others.

Each awkwardly takes a mug of tea.

JOSEPH. There are biscuits.

STEPHEN (*taking one*). Thank you.

Noise on the stairs. A crowd of CONGREGANTS, OFFICIALS, *etc. in suits, skirts, ecclesiastical robes, descends.*
A CHURCH PHOTOGRAPHER *slips in.*

PHOTOGRAPHER. Your Grace?

OFFICIAL. (Michael)

He lifts his camera.

OFFICIAL. Vicar! They're down here!
We found them.

DANIEL. Please. No.

PHOTOGRAPHER. It's just for our newsletter, it's just –

OFFICIAL. You're having tea…

DANIEL. *No.*

MICHAEL. Yes.

PHOTOGRAPHER (*lowering camera*). Oh.

DANIEL. Thank you.

PHOTOGRAPHER. Sorry. Right.

REVEREND FARLEY descends the stairs and peers in.

FARLEY. Excuse me.

DANIEL. Mr Farley.

FARLEY (*surprised*). Michael. Mark.

MICHAEL. Hello, Vicar.

JOSEPH *nods*.

FARLEY. Daniel – ?

DANIEL. We'll be up in a moment, Vicar. Thank you.

Little pause.

FARLEY. We are rather behind.

STEPHEN. Yes.

FARLEY. People are getting restless. I'm sorry.

DANIEL. We've got nine minutes yet. Don't we?

STEPHEN. Yes, you can begin as planned, George, thank you.
    We'll be there for our entrance, don't worry.

FARLEY. Good. Of course you will.
    Thank you. Good.

He turns back into the stairway. Polite nods from the
OFFICIALS *as they turn and follow him. As they ascend,*
murmured comments, questions:

OFFICIAL. (What's…)

OFFICIAL. (What if they're
    not ready?)

OFFICIAL. (Yes – there's no
    way.)

OFFICIAL. (Do you want
    me to make sure they
    come up?)

FARLEY. (Quiet. They'll be
    fine. It's all fine.)

OFFICIAL. (Why are they
    having tea?)

OFFICIAL. (Isn't that… the
    cleaner…?)

OFFICIAL. (One of the
    cleaners, I think)

PHOTOGRAPHER. (Why
    can't we take their
    picture?)

OFFICIAL. (He's much
    smaller than I imagined)

Pause.
MICHAEL *looks to* JOSEPH.

MICHAEL. I've told them.

JOSEPH. I heard.

STEPHEN. Well

JOSEPH. You did not tell me about this event upstairs.

MICHAEL (*to* STEPHEN *and* DANIEL). This isn't what it
looks like.

DANIEL. It looks comfy.

MICHAEL. (Not really)

JOSEPH. It is not bad, we are comfortable. We have a cooker, /
a little fridge, a campbed.

MICHAEL. He doesn't mean we, he means he. Him. Not me.

STEPHEN. Okay

JOSEPH. The TV is bad

MICHAEL. It's not really, Joseph

JOSEPH. It does not get anything

MICHAEL. It's terrestrial, I brought it from home. Why are you
wearing that?

JOSEPH. Michael has been a very big help.
I am lucky.

MICHAEL. I'm trying.

STEPHEN. Yes. I see.
Very good.

DANIEL. Farley knows about this?

MICHAEL. No –	JOSEPH. Yes.
Sort of – he knows Joseph is here a lot, he cleans.	
We got him a job, for now	But I am not a cleaner.
– he goes out.	
It's the best we / can do.	I do not want to be a cleaner

DANIEL. But he doesn't know you two are – ?

MICHAEL. We're not –
    No. No, we're not.
    Now.
    We're.
    I'm just helping Joseph.

    It's not really any of your
    business.

STEPHEN. No, it's not.
    However it's difficult.

MICHAEL. No. I know.
    Of course not.

JOSEPH. (No)

He stares at MICHAEL.

Yes.

DANIEL. Our churches
aren't hotels

DANIEL. Is he using you, Michael?

STEPHEN. Daniel

Little laugh, JOSEPH.

MICHAEL. Does it matter?

DANIEL. I think it does. Yes.   JOSEPH. (Because I am
                                        African?)

MICHAEL. Have you seen his scars?

STEPHEN. We have, Michael, yes –
    We have, Joseph. We have.

JOSEPH. I am not blackmailing him

STEPHEN. No. / (*To* MICHAEL.) Michael, you can't entirely
    blame yourself.

DANIEL. (Okay. Fine)

MICHAEL. Maybe not

JOSEPH. We are friends.

MICHAEL. I want to help him. We're friends, yes.

JOSEPH. We are using each other.

DANIEL. But he can't stay.

STEPHEN. That's true, Michael

MICHAEL. I know

DANIEL (*to* JOSEPH). How long has he been down here?

MICHAEL. It's only temporary

(Joseph, please)

JOSEPH. I am evolving skin over my eyeballs

DANIEL. Right

JOSEPH. It does not feel temporary

MICHAEL. We have to be careful

STEPHEN. Yes

DANIEL. Yes
Yes we do

JOSEPH. I have been very careful

MICHAEL. Yes, I know

JOSEPH. I am still here

MICHAEL. Yes, we can see that.
I mean thorough.
We have to be thorough.
That's what takes so long.
It takes a long time to put together a comprehensive case.

JOSEPH. 'My case', yes

MICHAEL. Yes, your 'case', your claim, this kind of asylum
claim is difficult, yes

JOSEPH. Slowly slowly catchee monkey.

Little pause.
Upstairs, a moment of shuffling as people are taking their seats.

MICHAEL. Yes.

DANIEL. Okay. Michael, look

MICHAEL. Please

DANIEL. Stephen

STEPHEN. What do you think we should do, Michael?

MICHAEL. Please

DANIEL (*to* STEPHEN). What do you think we should do, your Grace?

MICHAEL. I want to sort all this out as soon as I can, honestly. But we have to move so cautiously and be scrupulous and explore every option, because it's very complicated

STEPHEN. I understand that

DANIEL. (Please, Stephen)

MICHAEL. I'm speaking to lawyers; I'm speaking to experts. I'm speaking to people who have gone through what you've gone through, Joseph, trying to assemble the facts and evidence and figure out exactly what needs to be said, exactly what's expected and how it needs to be said in order to ensure you're successful – do you understand?
Because once you're in the system –

DANIEL. Michael

MICHAEL (*to* STEPHEN *and* DANIEL). You know this – once you're *in*, then you're in, and there are only two answers: yes or no. And that can be very, very fast, indeed.

DANIEL. Nonetheless, Michael. *Today*.

JOSEPH (*to* MICHAEL). But we have evidence.

MICHAEL (*to* JOSEPH).   DANIEL. We have to sort
Yes I know we do   this out today

JOSEPH (*indicating his scarred back*). We have evidence

DANIEL. Now

MICHAEL (*to* JOSEPH). But it's not enough.
Unfortunately. It's not.
(*To* DANIEL.) It's not

STEPHEN. Okay

JOSEPH. I think maybe we need a witness. Who gets up and speaks. Today. Maybe this / is what takes so long.

DANIEL. Sorry?

JOSEPH. This time it takes you to get it up

MICHAEL. Joseph   DANIEL. What did you say?

JOSEPH. To screw it up, / screw up your courage

MICHAEL (Stop it)   STEPHEN. Joseph, please.
                                   Let's discuss this calmly.
                                   Michael. Daniel.

JOSEPH. Decide your yes or no

MICHAEL. I don't know why I let you treat me like this

JOSEPH. Because you like it.

    It makes you feel better.

MICHAEL. Is that what you   DANIEL. (This is ridicu-
    think?   lous)

JOSEPH. That is why I am stuck down here.

MICHAEL. But I'm not a witness, Joseph, I wasn't there, I
    didn't see anything
    What do you want? I'm trying.
    What do you want me to say?

JOSEPH. You were there   DANIEL (*indicating upstairs
                                 with great concern*). Can
                                 we keep this down,
                                 please? Please.

MICHAEL. No, I wasn't, no
    Briefly, yes I was there briefly
    But I wasn't there when, was I
    When you were

JOSEPH. Beaten

MICHAEL. Yes

JOSEPH. No

MICHAEL. No, Joseph

STEPHEN. Joseph

JOSEPH. No. When I was beaten you were not there.

But if I point to this evidence and explain, Michael, I think
they will see one thing.
If *you* point to the evidence, point to me, if you explain in
your words what happened, how we met, how we fucked, /
how you left

DANIEL. Joseph!   MICHAEL. Joseph

STEPHEN. It's okay. / It's fine

JOSEPH. How you left and then what happened – they will see
something different.
Won't they?

MICHAEL. No.

JOSEPH. Yes, I think they will.

MICHAEL. Maybe.

JOSEPH. And if you say nothing –
Maybe it did not happen, right?

MICHAEL. No. That's not it.

JOSEPH. If nobody says anything.
And nobody is offended.

MICHAEL. You have to be patient.

JOSEPH. But not for ever.

Pause.

STEPHEN. We understand why you're upset, Joseph.
It's difficult.

Noise upstairs: dull announcements, etc., indecipherable.
JOSEPH *stares at* MICHAEL. *At the others.*

JOSEPH. I think we should go upstairs. / It sounds like it is starting

DANIEL. I don't think that's a good idea

MICHAEL. Come on, Joseph

JOSEPH. I would like to look at this window again. / I would like to see all the groups upstairs

STEPHEN. Yes, of course you would

DANIEL. No

JOSEPH. Maybe see this press scrum: is it 'scrum'? / 'Scum' or 'scrum'?

MICHAEL. (Joseph)

JOSEPH. Speak to *them*, maybe. Tell them why I am here.

DANIEL. Are you for real, Joseph? Is he for real?! What are you trying to do here? What do you *want*?

JOSEPH. I am not embarrassed.
Michael is not embarrassed.

He stares at DANIEL.

DANIEL. Michael looks embarrassed.

MICHAEL. (Please)

DANIEL. Are you on his side or our side?

MICHAEL. I'm not on anyone's side

DANIEL. Do you want to go upstairs, Michael?
Would you like to 'testify' up there today? With him.
Clear your conscience. Embarrass Stephen upstairs?

MICHAEL. I don't have an agenda, Daniel

STEPHEN. We know that

DANIEL. But you do have a wife who's expecting your child, don't you?

STEPHEN. Daniel, no

MICHAEL. Yes.

JOSEPH. She knows.

Little pause.

DANIEL. What?

STEPHEN. Does she?

DANIEL. She knows?   MICHAEL. No.
                                              Yes.

JOSEPH. She has met me

DANIEL. Really?

MICHAEL. She's *seen* you

DANIEL. Has she?

JOSEPH. She gave me a sandwich

STEPHEN. I see

MICHAEL. She *pitied* you, Joseph.
    Do you understand that? She didn't accept you.

He looks at him. JOSEPH *stares back.*

JOSEPH. Has she accepted you?

Little pause.
MICHAEL *turns to the others.*

MICHAEL. She knows. Yes.
    She doesn't *know*, doesn't want to know, but.
    We don't talk about it.

    She's due in eight weeks.
    She's very excited.

DANIEL. Has she kicked you out?

MICHAEL. No. We're married. We have a house. We're going
    to be parents.

*Noise upstairs – low whispers, etc.: the congregation
waiting.*

Pause.

I repulse her, of course
She doesn't say, but I know what she thinks, I'm her husband
Not the physical stuff
That's bad enough I'm sure, but.
The lies.
She's repulsed by the fact that the lies I tell aren't to save me
or to save her but
Any lie necessary to save us.
'Us.'

It's the ice that binds us.
I don't blame her.

Little pause.

I feel bad about everything.

Little laugh.

I'm trying to do right by everyone.

JOSEPH. That is impossible.

MICHAEL. Maybe   DANIEL. (Yes)

STEPHEN. No. We must look to God and ask His guidance
    every day.

JOSEPH. God asked Abraham to sacrifice his own son.
    Abraham was willing to do it.

MICHAEL. Joseph

JOSEPH. He wants to know what we would kill for him.

STEPHEN. That's a very severe interpretation.

JOSEPH. This is in the Bible too.

STEPHEN. But God intervened, Joseph. He didn't ruin
    Abraham's life. Or Isaac's. He substituted a ram.

JOSEPH. Yes, that is right.
    In the story everything turns out okay.
    But Abraham did not know that.

(*To* MICHAEL.) I would like to go upstairs now.

MICHAEL. (Joseph, please)

JOSEPH. I crossed the world to get here.
I am not embarrassed of anything I have done.
There are always consequences.

Upstairs the sound of the congregation rising to their feet.
JOSEPH *and* MICHAEL *look at one another for a long time.*

MICHAEL (*quietly*). I can't go upstairs with you, Joseph. I'm sorry.

Silence. JOSEPH *stares at* MICHAEL.

JOSEPH. No.

DANIEL. No.
Good.

STEPHEN. Joseph.

MICHAEL. (I'm sorry)

DANIEL (*to* STEPHEN). We're going to miss our cue.

STEPHEN. We do want to help you, Joseph. Really.
Please.
I'm looking you in the eye, Joe.

Tell me what you want.

Music begins upstairs.
JOSEPH *looks to* MICHAEL, *and then to* DANIEL, *who's fixing himself to leave – then to* STEPHEN.

Pause.

JOSEPH. I want to be safe.
I want a home.
A healthy, normal family.

STEPHEN. Very good.

JOSEPH. Then I want to be a bishop. Like you.

Pause. STEPHEN *frozen.*
Music rises.

DANIEL. (Let's go, Stephen.)

STEPHEN. Yes…
(*Small smile.*) God bless you both.

DANIEL (*to* MICHAEL *and* JOSEPH). Thank you for the tea.
Sorry to leave you to clean.

He ushers STEPHEN *towards the door, helps him with his vestments.*

The music rises.

DANIEL *and* STEPHEN *disappear upstairs.*

MICHAEL *and* JOSEPH *look at one another across the tea tray.*

Finally, MICHAEL *bends to clear up.*

JOSEPH *lifts his hand as if he might bless him – or strike him.*

MICHAEL. Don't.

Go.

He looks up into JOSEPH's *eyes – they stare at one another a moment.*

Upstairs, a robust choir joins the music: 'All Hail the Power of Jesus' Name.'

JOSEPH *turns, walks to the door leading upstairs. Looks back.*

He goes up the stairs.

MICHAEL *alone on his knees.*

The music plays on.